Wah DHONI!

Wah DHONI!

Arun Kumar Thakur

Vitasta
Let Knowledge Spread

Vitasta

Published by
Vitasta Publishing Pvt. Ltd.
2/15, Ansari Road, Daryaganj,
New Delhi - 110 002
info@vitastapublishing.com

ISBN: 978-93-80828-52-7

Cover & Layout Design by Vitasta Publishing Pvt. Ltd.
Printed by Vits Press, New Delhi

Marketed and Distributed exclusively in India & Sub-Continent by:

Times Group Books

Times Group Books
(A division of Bennett, Coleman and Company Limited)
Times Annexe, Express Building
9-10 Bahadur Shah Zafar Marg, New Delhi-110 002

To

My mother and my cricketing idols
M L Jaisimha and Nawab of Pataudi Jr

Contents

Acknowledgement

I am truly indebted to cricketers in Bihar and Jharkhand who had played with—or interacted with—Mahendra Singh Dhoni at various levels, including school, junior state, Ranji, Deodhar and other tournaments. They provided insights into his mind and game. I am equally indebted to various newspapers and television channels for their reports and analysis that enabled me to build a portrait of an exciting personality, not easy to fathom, because Team India's captain Dhoni personifies reticence. He guards his privacy with fierce determination.

Preface

How do you react to the meteoric rise of a person whom you have watched grow literally since his early teens? The way he tore into the Pakistani attack on 5 April 2005, at Vizag, for his first one-day international century, made me recollect that quiet and innocent looking school boy who first gave notice of his talent with an aggressive double century in less than 40 overs in the Ranchi District Inter School Final. He achieved what no one had done till then, neither his peers nor his seniors, in his home state. His inning against Pakistan made him a star overnight. The long mane, the freshness and the power behind his stroke plays made everyone sit up and take notice of this talent from Jharkhand, a state known for its mineral wealth rather than cricketers. Myths naturally followed him. Commentators started attributing the power behind his strokes to consumption of four litres of milk a day!

The moment he took off his shirt and gifted it to a young

fan after winning the inaugural ICC T-20 World Cup on 24 September 2007 at Johannesburg, in South Africa, and walked bare-chested towards the dressing room, he revealed yet another side of his personality. A new youth icon was born.

He has not looked back since then. Captain cool! Captain with the Midas touch! Commentators, including legendary Sunil Gavaskar, kept heaping praises on him. His achievements made me curious to know and understand the personality who grew in the cricketing backwaters of the cricket crazy country and captivated millions of cricket fans. Curiosity to understand the local boy, who made good in such a big way, led to this book. I hope it will help his fans understand MSD, or their Mahi, as he is called by his close relatives and friends. Mahi plays to win.

— Arun Kumar Thakur

1
Why This Book on Him?

When India won the ICC Cricket World Cup 2011 on the night of 2 April at the Wankhede Stadium, Dhoni received the trophy and then quietly left the centrestage to his teammates, who carried Sachin Tendulkar on their shoulders around the field. I received an SMS from Harsh Dev Sharan, a senior cardiologist, who is close to the family and has watched Dhoni grow as a man and as a cricketer, and one who follows the game seriously. He treats him like his son. The message read: "T20 world cup, 50 overs world cup, top ranking in test cricket, top ranking in ODI, 6000 runs in ODI, individual top ranking three times, what more can one achieve in just seven years. Isn't he the greatest ever? God bless Mahi."

On the night of 28 May, Dhoni added the Indian Premier League IV title to his cap. After receiving the cup he receded into the background once more.

Is he the greatest captain ever to have led Team India?

This is debatable, but Dhoni as a player, and particularly as a captain, fulfils the requirements of a good captain as suggested by none other than the legendary Don Bradman. In his book '*Art of Cricket*', Bradman said, "A good captain must be a fighter: confident but not arrogant, firm but not obstinate, able to take criticism without letting it unduly disturb him, for he is sure to get it–and unjustly too."

However, Dhoni as wicketkeeper-batsman-captain has proved even Bradman's views on captaincy wrong. Bradman held that to burden an allrounder, or a bowler, or a wicketkeeper with the added responsibility of captaincy was an unfair responsibility in the international field. His reasoning–"a wicketkeeper suffers from the disability that he must minutely concentrate on every ball, from the moment the bowler's run commences." Thus, in his view, "adding to that burden the task of captaincy is too much".

South Africa's batting genius Barry Richards too held views similar to those of Bradman. In case of Dhoni, he felt that as the wicketkeeper has to be on the ball all the time, it would not be possible to continue as wicketkeeper-captain for a long time. This view was expressed in 2007. Dhoni has continued as a wicketkeeper-captain for around four years now.

This is why former Pakistan captain and wicketkeeper Wasim Bari is so impressed with Dhoni. Bari said as a wicketkeeper-captain he found the job very difficult. But Dhoni has carried the responsibility of a captain, a wicketkeeper and a batsman well, at least thus far. He will complete seven years in the Indian team in December 2011.

Mahi, as Dhoni is fondly called by those close to him, has

come a long way since 23 December 2004, when he made his debut for India in an ODI against Bangladesh at Chittagong. It was not a happy debut. He was run out before he could open his account. In the next match he was caught while playing a pull shot. He could score only 19 runs in the three-Match series.

Yet he was picked up for the home ODI series, 2005, against Pakistan. He did not do much in the first match. His friends back home were worried. Was their Mahi going to fade away? Was his style of batting not suitable for that level of cricket? Or, was he just unlucky? If so, when would Lady Luck smile on him?

All these questions were answered in the second ODI, played on 5 April 2005, at Visakhapatnam. In what, some may describe as a providential intervention, captain Saurav Ganguly asked him if he would like to bat at number three. Maybe Sourav, not in the best of form then, was not keen to bat at number three and face the Pakistani fast bowlers when they were fresh. But to Dhoni it provided a great opportunity. He loves batting early in the order.

Mahi readily agreed. And when Sachin Tendulkar fell in the fourth over, out walked Mahi, in his trade mark brisk manner. He must have perceived that finally Lady Luck was starting to smile on him as he had always been more successful as a batsman and scored more runs when he batted up the order.

He kept that personal record intact. If the Pakistani fast bowlers thought they had another wicket, in the shape of a rookie, in their kitty, they were to be soon disillusioned. Attacking from the word go, he bludgeoned the Pak fast bowlers into meek submission to score 148 runs off 123 balls. He hit four sixes and 15 fours. A new cricketing icon had announced his arrival on the big stage.

In that innings he overshadowed Virendra Sehwag, who too scored a blistering 74 runs off 40 balls. That proved correct what Pradeep Khanna, an India under-25 and Duleep trophy wicketkeeper and batsman from Ranchi had said in December 2004, soon after Dhoni's selection: "When Dhoni will get going, fans will forget the likes of Sehwag and Sachin, he is such a big hitter of the cricket ball."

Next day, both the teams landed at the Ranchi airport en route to Jamshedpur, where the next ODI was to be played on April 9. The teams were to travel by road to Jamshedpur. Thousands of fans greeted the teams. It appeared as if all young people of the city had assembled there. Shouts of "Dhoni" and "Dhoni Bhaiya" drowned the roar of the aeroplanes.

Shouting "Dhoni bhaiya, Dhoni bhaiya", more than a hundred young boys chased the Indian team bus on their motorcycles. The chase continued for about 30-km on National Highway 33, just for a glimpse of their hero, a local boy who had made it big and had become a star. This writer was assigned to follow the teams with a photographer to cover and report if something funny or interesting happened between Ranchi and Jamshedpur.

All along that route fans and local residents stood in hordes to welcome the teams. For security reasons, the original route was changed some 30 or 40-km away from Jamshedpur.

Our car was right behind Team India's bus, with only a Sumo, carrying policemen, in between. The Sumo's brief was not to let any motorcycle come anywhere near the team buses. That Sumo kept swerving from extreme left to extreme right to prevent motorcycle-borne fans from getting alongside the bus. The persistent but crazy fans too kept swerving their motorcycles, and many a time a few of those motorcycles came on the verge of hitting either the Sumo or our car. We asked the driver to be careful and keeping our fingers crossed, watched with gaping mouths a live demonstration of how crazy and wild, cricket fans could get.

However, despite our crossed fingers, our worst fears came true when one motorcycle lost its balance on the highway. The two boys on it had almost succeeded in getting close to the Indian team's bus. But the Sumo swerved extreme left, and the two boys went down with their motorcycle while trying to avoid getting hit by the police vehicle. We stopped to see if the boys needed help. Fortunately, we were spared the decision of whether to help the boys, or ignore them and continue following the buses as assigned. The boys got up and limped towards their fallen motorcycle. They were lucky to have fallen into a grassy ditch. They had put their lives at stake for a mere glimpse of their hero. That's how crazy fans can get.

Perhaps, if the cricket authorities had arranged for a raised platform and allowed the fans a view of both Indian and Pakistani players, including the local boy and hero of the Vizag match, Dhoni, that mad motorcycle chase could have been avoided.

However, in the match at Jamshedpur, Dhoni did not score many runs. But his star value had already emerged. Spectators started leaving the stadium soon after he got out for 20 odd runs when he tried to pull a short rising ball from outside the off stump, which ended in a top edged catch. India went on to lose that match.

In 2006, India toured Pakistan. Dhoni, with his long mane and aggressive batting style, captivated the Pakistani cricket fans. Pakistan's then president Parvez Musharraf was so impressed that he went out of the way at the post match presentation ceremony to comment on his long mane, and advised him to "keep it that way as it suits you."

What is remarkable about Dhoni's personality, is that whatever hairstyle he tries, it suits him, as if he were made to sport that style! In the wee hours of 3 April 2011, while the World Cup victory celebrations were going on, he had his head shaved. The next morning everyone was taken aback to see a bald Dhoni- bald but still looking smart.

He prefers T-shirts and jeans, but looks equally comfortable and smart in a suit and tie. Put him on a stage with cine stars of the stature of Shah Rukh Khan and he looks completely at ease.

Team India may be under tremendous pressure, even on the verge of a defeat, but his face does not betray any negative emotion, or for that matter any emotion at all. With a shrug of his shoulders, a jerk of his head to his left, and a few blinks of his eyes, he takes his position behind the stumps to wait for the next ball. He has proved his critics wrong time and again. He has stuck to his decisions steadfastly, ignored the barbs thrown by former cricketers and experts; he supports his teammates and remains unruffled, cool, and calm. Confidence oozes out of every step he takes on the cricket field.

What stuff is he made of? What has made him what he is today? How did he manage to overcome the lack of infrastructural support to become an international star? Is he as cool within as he looks on the field?

This book is an attempt–a humble one at that, one must add–at unravelling the phenomenon that MSD or Dhoni, or Mahi has become–an attempt that was made difficult because of the central figure of this book, who personifies reticence. Even his friends and those close to him have begun to avoid saying anything on record, particularly to anyone from the media.

Hopefully, his fans will be able to find answers to those questions in the pages that follow.

***

2 Early Days in Cricket

When he walked out to open the innings for his school team, DAV Shyamali, in the finals of the inter-school tournament against Kendriya Vidyalaya, Hinoo, organized by Ranchi District Cricket Association at Harmu ground, he may not have known he was walking out to open a new chapter in his life. That was in February 1997. He was then four months away from his sixteenth birthday.

Together with Shabbir Hussain he put on a record 378 runs, his personal contribution being a double century, 213 runs in 137 balls with 26 boundaries and seven sixes. That was a 40-overs-a-side match!

That performance prompted Dr Harsh Dev Sharan to suggest his name to one of the selectors of the senior district team.

His selection was preceded by a long discussion, as some selectors took the stand that the Ranchi District Cricket Association rules and precedence permitted only a senior division player for selection to the senior district team. Even a B division player was not eligible, then how could one select a school boy. One of the selectors argued, "He is obviously talented and would benefit from exposure at that level, and we can include him in the 15, so that he can get used to senior cricket in the company of the senior players." Finally, the committee included him. He became the first school boy to be inducted in a team comprising half a dozen Ranji trophy players; some current and former Ranji players were left out. He did justify the argument of that selector. Once in the senior district team he went from strength to strength.

Among Indians, it is a widely held belief, that good deeds of a father visit upon his progenies. In Dhoni's case, this axiom proved very true. Pan Singh, Dhoni's father, who was a keen football fan, rendered a great service to cricket. He was in charge of water supply system at Mecon and its colony, known as Shyamali. When the Mecon management decided to build its stadium and prepare a turf wicket (the first in the city), the city was facing a water crisis; water supply was rationed in that residential area. The city was tense following Indira Gandhi's assassination. It was very difficult to maintain water supply for the newly laid turf and the ground but Pan Singh worked hard and managed sufficient water supply. The result was that Mecon could prepare a cricket ground for the match, which Bengal failed to win narrowly. A cash reward was given to the groundsman and curator UK Jena.

The Mecon stadium went on to host more than 16 Ranji matches, including the Ranji Trophy quarter finals between Bihar and Hyderabad in 1990-91 and then Bihar versus Karnataka in November 2002.

In the match against Karnataka, MSD scored a duck in the first innings, trapped by the left arm spin of Sunil Joshi, but made amends by scoring 93 runs in the second innings against the likes of Venkatesh Prasad, Doda Ganesh and SB Joshi — all three Indian players. His fans sighed when he fell seven short of his century. If he had completed the ton, it would have been a century scored in his own backyard, as his house was then just a furlong from the stadium, both located in Shyamali Colony.

However, those who had seen Pan Singh's dedication in providing water for preparing the Mecon wicket and ground, like Debal Sahay, who was the then incharge of Mecon cricket, believed strongly that God has rewarded Pan Singh through his son Dhoni.

But, ironically, though Dhoni was born in Shyamali and his father worked in Mecon, he never actually played for the Mecon cricket team, which was one of the best teams in the state. Instead he began his career in league matches in 1994-95 with Commandos. He played for Research and Development Centre for Iron and Steel, Central Coalfields Limited, and South Eastern Railway. However, after an unsuccessful tour of Sri Lanka in 2006, he practised at Mecon stadium to regain his form.

Among those teams, clearly the four year stint with the Central Coalfields Limited was the most productive. He toured the country playing in different tournaments that provided the much needed exposure.

But very few remember, and even MSD fails to mention his

first cricketing tour, in 1996, when he was all of 15. He made the trip to Delhi as a member of the Bihar Under-16 squad for the All India School Cricket tournament for the Vinoo Mankad Trophy, which is organised by the School Games Federation of India. He played as a wicketkeeper and batted at No. 10. Playing against Gujarat, and batting at No.10, he scored six not out in his team's total of 105, all out in 32.4 overs. Bihar lost that match by five wickets.

Not only that, playing for CCL as a stipend player, he did not have to worry about bat and other cricketing gears. All these were taken care of, with a healthy stipend of Rs 2,200 per month to boot. That helped him indulge in his passion for motorcycles. Starting with a Rajdoot, he moved on to an Enfield Bullet, which suited his build and passion. Today he owns 23 motorcycles, including a Harley Davidson.

***

3
Dhoni and Deities

The temple of Deori Mata, one of the various forms of Goddess Kali, is about 50-km from Ranchi. It is a must stop for most cricketers travelling to Jamshedpur. For Team India captain MSD too, the Deori Mata temple is a must visit destination whenever he is in the city, in between his cricketing and advertisement commitments. Before the World Cup 2011, he was home only for a day or two in February. But he took time out to visit the temple to offer prayers.

And on 3 April 2011, after Team India won the World Cup, some of his close friends visited the temple as thanksgiving for his success. Incidentally, MSD got the news of Rajiv Gandhi Khel Ratna award, on 4 August 2008, when he was leaving the Deori temple premises after offering his prayers.

On most of his visits to the temple, he is accompanied by his close friends, and in recent times his new friend, Sudesh Mahto, the Jharkhand sports minister.

He had an early exit from the World Cup, 2007, when he failed with the bat both against Bangladesh and in the do-or-die match against Sri Lanka. He walked in against Bangaldesh and tried to hit a left arm spinner and ended up giving a simple catch to gully. Against Sri Lanka, he was foxed by Muralitharan's wiles and was trapped leg before wicket to a fast and straight delivery from round the wicket. He failed to open his account.

Following those nightmarish batting performances, he spent some time in his hometown in April 2007. Then, besides Deori Temple, he visited the famous Rajrappa temple in Ramgarh, which is one of the 51 known Shakti peeths in the country. He also offered prayers at the Delbera temple of Lord Shiva in Silli. That must have helped restore his confidence because later that year he was made vice captain for the Ireland, Scotland and England tour, and captain of Team India for the first T20 World Cup in South Africa. As a captain, he has not looked back since winning the T20 World Cup.

His first visit to the Deori temple was in 1999, when he went on motorcycle with his friends to offer prayers before the Ranji trials, recalls one of his mentors Chanchal Bhattacharya. That was the year he made it to the Bihar Ranji team and in the very first match against Assam at Keenan Stadium in Jamshedpur, announced his arrival. Batting at number seven, he scored 44 and a not out 68. This was also the season when he made his presence felt in the under-19 teams of the state, the East zone and the rest of India.

Experts say this temple dates back to the 8th century. Folklore has it that the king of Tamar saw a dream, in which he was asked to locate this temple hidden somewhere in the forest and start offering prayers there. The reigning goddess here is the 16-armed version of Goddess Durga. While preserving the original form and location of the Goddess, the building of this temple is being expanded.

In recent times this temple has gained in popularity. The priests there, like Manoj Panda, have become much sought after by the media. Frequently they are seen on news channels giving sound bytes on Dhoni. Its fame and appeal has spread far and wide as inadvertently MSD has become its brand ambassador. Now those in distress believe that if they offer prayers there, all their problems will be solved and their wishes fulfilled.

In fact, after India won the World Cup on 2 April, footfalls at the temple increased manifold from next morning itself. An obviously happy Manoj Panda said around 2000 people were coming in from different corners of the state.

A recount of his early days in cricket will explain his faith and devotion to the Deori Temple, in particular, and other temples as well. He has had so many narrow escapes from slipping into anonymity that only supreme faith kept him motivated and pushed him to pursue his dream of playing for India.

When he was first selected to represent the East Zone team in 2000, he got the news of his selection very late — that too through a Calcutta based friend who read of his selection in a newspaper. His brother-in-law Gautam Gupta and some close friends helped him hire a car to Calcutta so that he could join the team before it flew to Agartala. When he reached Calcutta, the team had left. It was sheer luck that a Ranchi based athletic coach HR Das had a friend who helped him get a seat on the next flight. He just made it in time, otherwise he would have suffered the ignominy of not reporting. This episode also reveals how cricket is administered at the zone and state level, where a player gets to know of his selection through indirect channel and, at times, such information reaches very late. It is anybody's guess how many talented cricketers may have missed out because of such shoddy administration.

Earlier, when he jumped straight from school cricket into the senior district cricket team, it was a lucky break as the selection committee accepted the arguments advanced in his favour by one of the selectors.

At the selection trials for the under-19 state team 1998-99 at Jamshedpur, he remained padded for an entire day as the selectors ignored his presence. Luckily an official from the district intervened and he was asked to bat. Naturally, after seeing him bat, the selectors could not ignore him.

He and his close friends may thank divine intervention on 5 April 2005, at Visakhapattnam against Inzamam–ul-Haq's Pakistan team. Promoted to number three by captain Sourav Ganguly, he scored 148 runs off 123 balls with 12 fours and 4 sixes. He had cemented his place in the Indian ODI team.

On the tour of Sri Lanka, an uninspiring performance both with the bat and behind the stumps, raised doubts about his form. But he returned home, and launched into serious practice at Mecon stadium. He bounced back as Dinesh Karthik, wicketkeeper-batsman, did not capitalize on the chances that came his way during that phase.

The devotion to the deity and these early narrow escapes explain why MSD appears so cool and calm on and off the field, even while the commentators and experts appear worried.

Right from day one as captain, he has given the impression that he understands that success and failure go together. On several occasions he has said that "the players ought to enjoy their cricket" and not put pressure on themselves by worrying about the result of a match. This perhaps is the key to that wonderful and relaxed atmosphere in the dressing room, which made even a player like Sachin Tendulkar talk glowingly about the 'dressing room atmosphere'.

Indeed, when the dressing room was vitiated during Greg Chappell's tenure as the coach of Team India, Sachin felt stifled and struggled to give his best.

He appears to believe strongly in the teaching of *Shrimad Bhagvadgita* (the *Gita*) that one should do one's work with sincerity and dedication and leave the result to God.

This does not mean that he does not get angry and is indifferent to a loss; far from it. He may outwardly appear calm and indifferent in the face of defeat, but that calm exterior hides a churning volcano within.

MSD says he does get angry but knows that giving vent to anger is not necessarily going to help.

The most noticeable expression of his anger was when some reports appeared about the selection of Team India, wherein it was reported that Dhoni had rooted for the left arm fast bowler Rudra Pratap Singh.

Dhoni retorted sarcastically that it would better to telecast the proceedings of the selection committee proceedings live, instead of someone leaking the details to the media.

His Ranji team mates-cum- friends, like Santosh Lal and Shabbir Hussain say he gets angry, though he may hide it on most occasions. They say MSD does not like to lose a match. Once he refused to have lunch as the CCL team had lost the match in a tournament at Muri. Win he must but using fair means.

Once, in a match at Lucknow, playing for the Central Coalfields Limited team, he was declared man of the match but his team had lost the match. He accepted the award calmly, but smashed it to pieces once he returned to the room where the players were staying. His stand was that the award was of no value as the match had been lost. In another incident he smashed his bat so hard against a drain, (after a loss), that it broke into pieces!

On the field when a player slackens, MSD chides him in a sarcastic tone. As he said in an interview to an electronic news channel, "I am sarcastic". In one of the ODIs in Australia in 2008, he was heard shouting at a fielder who was sluggish on that one ball, "*sone ke liye kaafi waqt milega*" (wake up! You will get enough time to sleep after the match).

Yet he is a mature young man, who is reticent, and who manages to keep his emotions hidden, at least most of the times.

Of the rare occasions when he was visibly excited and showed his emotions, three come readily to mind.

The first, and most recent, was when Team India won the World Cup, 2011, at Wankhede stadium. His eyes welled up with tears though he turned his back to the cameras.

Earlier, in 2007, after Team India won the first edition of T20 World Cup in South Africa, MSD took off his shirt and gave it to a young fan. He remained in a sleeveless T-shirt through out the presentation ceremony.

The third was at Dharamshala in the third edition of Indian Premier League, when his power packed performance propelled Chennai Super Kings to victory from a hopeless situation. After the winning runs were scored he pumped his hands in a manner that he rarely does.

This form of MSD was visible at Wankhede stadium on 2 April evening too. He walked in to bat ahead of Yuvaraj Singh and hit a blistering 91 not out in 79 balls, and lofted Nuwan Kulasekara for a six to win the match and the World Cup for India with balls to spare.

Incidentally, at the awards presentation ceremony at Wankhede stadium too he was seen in a sleeveless T-shirt, as while receiving the T20 World Cup in 2007. A strange coincidence that!

***

4
Dhoni's Unique Batting Technique

Dhoni has baffled cricket pundits with his unique style of batting. When he hit those sixes against Pakistan on 5 April 2005, at Vizag, what everyone noticed, and what mystified everyone was how his bat rotated at the completion of his powerful lofted shots. That rotation resembled the rotation of the blades of a helicopter. It came to be described as the 'helicopter shot'.

When he played the helicopter shots he reminded one of ancient warriors: long hair fanning out from beneath the helmet and standing tall on his toes with the bat swirling over his head, surrounded by eleven enemies. An ancient warrior was swirling a mace to annihilate the enemy. He did it with a cricket bat and annihilated the opponent.

This shot is the result of MSD's participation in canvas ball cricket, or some would say tennis ball cricket, which he played since he was 12. He used to play in as many canvas ball cricket tournaments as he could, which earned him plenty of pocket money too. He was so popular on the tennis ball circuit for his big hitting that some teams paid him Rs 2000 to play for them.

The compulsion of that brand of cricket was to score as many runs as possible in six or ten overs as the number of overs varied from tournament to tournament.

But there used to be a bonus. For each four or six the batsman would get Rs 100. "He was very popular in the colliery areas for his sixes and aggressive batting. He must have played in all collieries and collected huge amounts," recalls Debal Sahay, former player and a senior cricket administrator.

Once, at the CCL's Gandhi Nagar colony Sahay, then director (personnel), was invited to be the chief guest at a night game of canvas ball tournament. "I was there on time, around 7 pm, by which time the final match was expected to be over. But when I reached there I found that the match had not even started. The spectators had held up the match because Dhoni had not arrived. When he arrived on the pillion of a rickety scooter, he apologized saying he got delayed because the match he was playing in was delayed".

This incident reminds one of Sachin Tendulkar's early days when his coach Ramakant Achrekar used to carry him from one match to the other so that Sachin could get maximum batting practise in match situations. Coaches and players know that an innings in a match is worth hours spent at the nets.

To get back to MSD's 'helicopter shot', it was innovated by MSD and his friend Santosh Lal in order to maximize runs from every ball in a canvas ball match, revealed his brother-in-law

Gautam. When the bowlers tried to bowl yorkers to prevent from going over the boundary, he countered by digging into the shot with a slight backward shuffle and lofted the ball powerfully. This shot ended in such a flourish that the fast and powerful swing of the bat created a momentum of its own and circumscribed a couple of circles at the end of the follow through.

Though MSD plays this shot very infrequently these days, as he has taken upon himself the task of providing solidity to the middle order, it bounced back into limelight through a cold drink advertisement during World Cup 2011.

Otherwise, if you look closely at his technique, you will notice that he grips the bat strongly with his right hand and when he hits the ball through covers, or to long on, he is able to generate tremendous power. Commentators have frequently described his powerful cover drives, mostly off the back foot, as "clobbering the ball" in a manner that reminds us of a powerful forehand shot by a tennis player; or, as if a powerful woodcutter is wielding an axe. Cine star John Abraham, a close friend of MSD, once said that when he asked him how to grip a bat, MSD advised him to pick it up like one picks up an axe. Some clue to his sledge hammer shots!

As far as power behind his shots is concerned, two shots remain vivid in memory. One was a straight hit over the sight screen during that match winning knock of 183 runs against Sri Lanka. The other was a hook off the Pakistan's leading pace bowler Shoaib Akhtar in a Test match in Pakistan (2005). He swayed back a bit and hooked an Akhtar bouncer off his face with such ferocity that it must have dented the bowler's confidence.

He may lack the grace and fluidity of a Brian Lara, or the technical perfection of a Sunil Gavaskar, but if you look closely you will find that he uses short back lift while defending, and tries to move his front foot as close to the line of ball as possible. As he is a powerful and fast runner between the wickets, he keeps the strike rotating and the scoreboard moving.

MSD admits that these days he tries to settle down first. This means he stays calm and concentrates on ones and twos before taking charge. A correct approach! Legendary master technician Sunil Gavaskar advises a batsman to give the bowlers the first half an hour and the rest of the day will belong to him, the batsman.

Besides that, in any ball game including cricket, 'ball sense' is a prerequisite. And in cricket 'hand-eye' is the key to stroke making, like in the case of Virendra Sehwag, who makes up his lack of footwork with balance and the hand-eye co-ordination. These days the bat speed too is a frequently used term. Powerful wrists and forearms help MSD generate bat speed. His batting technique includes all these attributes.

To cap all these is the added quality that he is a fast learner. In the World Cup 2007 Muralitharan foxed him to trap him lbw. In the Asian Cup final, Ajantha Mendis trapped him.

But in the World Cup, 2011, final at Wankhede stadium, MSD promoted himself ahead of the in-form Yuvraj Singh. The confident walk to the crease, and the glint in his eyes made his fans and kith and kin back home feel that he would do something special. And he did.

That was not a decision prompted by some gut feeling, or

whim. That was a decision taken on sound cricketing logic. MSD himself said that when the third wicket fell, two off spinners, Muralitharan and Randive were operating. Left handed Gautam Gambhir was at the crease and another left handed batsman Yuvraj Singh would have made the task of the two off spinners easier. Besides that, courtesy three seasons in IPL in which Murli plays for MSD led Chennai Super Kings, MSD now reads him better than before.

Hence the confidence that he would be able to prevent Murli from dominating the proceedings. Was that not a good cricketing decision? MSD scored 91 unbeaten runs to win the match with a man of the match award!

***

5
Dhoni and Jharkhand

MSD is spoilt for choice. If he desires he can live in Chennai, Mumbai, Delhi, or Mussourie. He can set up his home at any of these places, or elsewhere. But he considers Ranchi his home. It is a remarkable aspect of his character that he has remained loyal to the city and the state where he was born and where he grew up as a cricketer. Though at one stage, senior cricketers felt he should move to some major cricket playing state if he was keen to play for India.

"I love Ranchi and I love Jharkhand, can't live anywhere else," he had told this writer in August 2007. Then he was vice captain to Rahul Dravid and was about to be given the captaincy of the Indian team for the inaugural T20 World Cup in South Africa.

"Ranchi is not a small city really. It is a cosmopolitan city where people from every part of the country have settled. We find people, from different religions and communities living here," he had said.

He added, "I think roads are very important. We should plan things, especially the roads. It's a capital city; lots of people come in and will come in. That is why the city needs alternative roads, flyovers, 5-Star Hotels, and big malls". This reveals that MSD, (unlike many other sportsmen who think of nothing beyond their chosen sport and rewards), is not only focused on his cricketing career, but also nurses a vision for the city where he was born.

He has a vision for the state of Jharkhand too. "We are the richest in mineral resources and we really need to expand implementing those MoUs, and the amount of money floating in will help in providing better educational and medical facilities".

Though not a graduate, he thinks like an economist and a planner when he stresses that roads are very important for the growth of a city and a state.

What he lacked as an upcoming player, he now seeks to provide for those who aspire for national and international recognition in sports. That is why he has followed up his loyalty to the city and the state with a project for a sports academy, where besides cricket, youngsters will get coaching in football, hockey and some other games.

MSD, therefore, wants to establish a sports academy. He has already had talks with chief minister Arjun Munda, sports minister Sudesh Mahto and the Central Coalfields Limited chairman-cum-managing director R K Saha.

He must have been happy to learn that as a reward for winning the World Cup, 2011, both the chief minister and the sports minister have announced a five acre plot for his sports academy.

But as the sports academy would need 15 acres, his team, that will look after the project, are hoping that the state government's five acre plot is so located that they can purchase, if need be, the additional ten acres, his brother-in-law Gautam reveals.

"The CCL management, on its part, is ready to provide financial aid for the cricket coaching wing of the proposed academy. But the aid will also depend on the proposal that comes from him," says Adil Hussain, manager(sports), CCL, who incidentally was captain of the company's cricket team when MSD was a part of the team.

He has also founded a Mahendra Singh Dhoni Charitable Trust with Rhiti Sports Management group, with whom he signed a contract in July 2010 for looking after his endorsements.

In 2007 itself he thought of a sports academy. Then he had said, "We have players, in hockey, in cricket, and other games. We need to give them infrastructure. Then only they can rise higher because it's so competitive. It's so tough." Perhaps, as a player who overcame odds to reach the top he was concerned to do something for upcoming players of the state.

So far as MSD Charitable Trust is concerned, its first visible effort was seen on Sakshi's (Dhoni's wife) second visit to her husband's birthplace, on 28 November 2010, a Sunday. Accompanied by her father-in-law Pan Singh, Sakshi distributed blankets among the rural poor of Thakurgaon, Patratoli and Kopretan villages so that they could have a warm winter.

This was followed by a T20 cricket tournament at the upcoming international cricket stadium of Jharkhand State Cricket Association at Dhurwa, in the Heavy Engineering

Corporation township. The purpose behind this tournament was to find talented youngsters and help them with coaching facilities either at home, or abroad.

That is Dhoni. Despite his busy cricket and advertisements schedule, he does think of his city and state, and players who need support.

Indeed, there had come a stage in his cricketing career when seniors suggested that he should move to some other state, like Bengal or Delhi, if he wanted to represent the country.

Former Test wicketkeeper Syed Saba Karim is an example. While playing for Bihar he was selected for the Indian team's tour of the West Indies in 1989. Dilip Vengsarkar was the captain. Saba returned home without playing in any Test. He was dumped from the team too. Then he shifted to Bengal and was, rewarded with a regular place in Team India. He went on to tour South Africa and other countries before a freak accident injured one of his eyes in an India-Bangladesh match and forced him to retire prematurely from international cricket. But the fact remains that Saba had to shift to West Bengal to bounce back in reckoning.

Hence, credit should be given to MSD that he refused to move away from Jharkhand. He could have shifted to Delhi or Kolkata. Instead, he held the ground that he would continue to play for Jharkhand. This stand of his was remarkable because in 2004 he performed consistently for the India A team in the triangular series in Kenya. He scored two back to back centuries against a Pakistan A team, comprising some Test players, and another 71 odd runs to win two man of the match awards. Even then he and his friends were not sure if he would get a call for the senior Indian Team. His friends were desperately seeking advice as to what he should do to get short listed by the national selectors.

The much desired call came and he was picked up for the One day international series in Bangladesh. He did not do very well there, run out off the first ball, and seven odd runs in the second match, before holding out to midwicket. On this dismissal he had said, "I got caught as I wanted to keep that pull shot down. If I had wanted to go over the top I would have cleared it." In that dismissal too he had discerned a cricketing lesson.

Anyway, what is apparent is that despite so many tempting options, MSD remains loyal to city where he was born and brought up. And cricket fans have responded well too, going crazy with enthusiasm whenever he does well, and when he returns home. Fans keep vigil at his home, wait patiently for hours, just to get a glimpse of him.

The state too has responded well. His house Shaurya is built on a plot gifted by the state government. He bought a smaller plot adjacent to it so that he could build his dream house..

Fans too have remained loyal to him. When he got married on 4 July 2010 at Dehradun, fans kept thronging the airport and his home in Harmu Housing colony hoping to get a glimpse of Mr and Mrs MSD.

It was on 7 July 2010, Dhoni's birthday that they lifted their vigil — that too after Mr and Mrs Dhoni appeared on the balcony and acknowledged the fans' greetings. He had arrived the same forenoon from Delhi with his bride. And like many other occasions, Dhoni succeeded in hoodwinking the media and he and Sakshi were whisked away from the airport. Still, a persistent media followed him and captured the newly weds on the balcony.

Dhoni spent his 29th birthday with his family and close friends and left for Calcutta, where his in-laws live.

But as everyone has realized now, confidence in his own ability is his forte. This has helped him in fulfilling his dream for playing for India while staying in Jharkhand, whose Ranji team is yet to play in the Elite group of Ranji Trophy.

***

6
Dhoni in 2007

The year 2007, will stand out as that year in MSD's life and career when his fortunes fluctuated wildly.

It sank to dismal depths in the early part of the year. In the second half of the same year he rose like a Phoenix to attain dizzy heights of success.

In August that year he was named captain of Team India for the T20 World Cup in South Africa. Senior players including Sachin Tendulkar had decided not to participate in that tournament. The selectors were looking for a captain as Yuvraj Singh and Virendra Sehwag were not a certainty, one because of fitness and the other because of form. Moreover, MSD was already Rahul Dravid's deputy then.

Sachin Tendulkar suggested Dhoni's name as he had perceived that "he had situational awareness of the game". The BCCI agreed with his suggestion. The rest, as they say, is history.

Before landing in South Africa, India had played only one T20 match against South Africa. Thus, the Indian players were unfamiliar with this new format. Experts too did not give them any chance. But India won the Cup defeating Pakistan in the final at Johannesburg. This was in September 2007, the second half of the year.

But the month of March that year was horrific for Indian cricket. In the World Cup 2007 in the West Indies, Team India was first defeated by Bangladesh, and in a do or die match by Sri Lanka. In both these matches India's strong batting line up, comprising Sachin Tendulkar, Rahul Dravid and Sourav Ganguly, failed to get past the 200 mark. Unfortunately, Dhoni did not open his account in either of those two matches.

Ugly incidents across the country reminded one all over again of the fickleness of cricket fans in the country. When Ajit Wadekar, replaced the late Nawab of Pataudi as captain, because of then chairman of selection committee Vijay Merchant's casting vote, and went on to lead India to its first ever series win over the West Indies, led by Sir Gary Sobers, in their own den, in 1970-71, he was hailed as a great captain. It was the series in which Sunil Gavaskar had made his debut and in four of the five Tests that he played he scored a record 772 runs.

In 1972, when Wadekar led India to its first ever series win, 1-0, winning the Oval Test courtesy leg spinner Chandrasekhar's five wickets and Eknath Solkar's miraculous catches at short leg, against England in England, his greatness was confirmed.

But two years later, after the 1974 tour of England, he had become a hated man. On this tour India were bowled out for

42 runs, and the Indian team returned home defeated, and humiliated. Fans pelted stones at Wadekar's statue. He was forced to step down, and for the West Indies tour of India in 1974 the late Nawab of Pataudi was requested to take over the captaincy.

Again, when the Indian team began the ICC World Cup 2003 in South Africa with some losses, fans back home gave violent expression to their disappointment, and pelted stones at homes of players like Md Kaif. However, India won four of its five matches to reach the final. It is another story that in the final, played at Johannesburg, Australian batsmen trampled over the Indian bowlers to win by 125 runs.

In March 2007 too, ugly incidents were reported from across the country, including Bangalore, home town of captain Rahul Dravid, soon after India lost to Sri Lanka and made an early exit from the World Cup, 2007.

Dhoni's home city, Ranchi, too figured in telecasts by some news channels. Though it is a different matter, that in his home city the backlash was stage managed. Nevertheless, visuals of fans burning posters and felling a temporarily arranged wall of bricks left an indelible impression on MSD and his family vis-a-vis the media.

Years later, Dhoni, maintaining his familiar stoic calm, admitted that the backlash after the loss in the World Cup, 2007, in the West Indies, had left him depressed for a month.

Those incidents still rankle him. So much so that four years later, after winning the World Cup, 2011, MSD happened to see a news clip on television that showed a huge crowd of fans, in front of his house in Harmu colony celebrating India's win.

He remarked that it was kind of funny that so many fans were there at his house.

Later, he commented, as reported in India Today, "When we win a game I don't go around beating my fans, saying that you bashed my house in 2007. Fans should be with you when you are not doing well."

In 2007, his home city some overzealous media personnel went overboard in organizing the protests against MSD. In a neatly organized move, at his under-construction house at Harmu Housing Colony, bricks surrounding a pillar under construction were felled by the youth wing of Jharkhand Mukti Morcha. At Albert Ekka Chowk, the instigated protestors were provided with enlarged copies of his photographs downloaded from internet. They burnt his portrait and also performed mock last rites. Along with visuals from other cities these visuals too were telecast across the country, though a day later a section of Youth Congress workers too claimed their share on the news channels by restoring the felled bricks. This too was, of course, duly recorded and telecast. But by this time irreparable damage had been done.

Since that day, the doors of the Dhoni's home have remained shut to the media. No one from his family gives any byte to the electronic medium or a statement to the print medium.

Their aversion to media has become such that once two scribes from a Bengali newspaper managed to sneak into their drawing room with a group of school teachers. Gautam, Dhoni's brother-in-law, spotted them after one of them pulled out his notebook. Both were ushered out politely.

On other occasions too the media has been kept at arm's length. Some reporters complained that they had spent hours in front of his new house in Harmu colony on the day the grihapravesh (house warming) puja was being performed. Dhoni had not come for that puja. Yet, no media person was allowed inside, what hurt some of them was that after the puja was over, prasad was distributed to the guards, but that courtesy was not extended to the waiting media personal.

Also, when members of his family returned after MSD's wedding on 4 July 2010, at Dehradun, the media was waiting for them, expecting that the bridegroom and the bride too would be there.

MSD and Sakshi, however, did not come with the family. Still, all that the media got were a few shots of his parents, sister Jayanti, brother-in-law Gautam and the couple of selected friends who had been invited to Dehradun. But no one spoke to the media.

A couple of days before the ICC World Cup 2011 final at Wankhede, when a reporter and a photographer approached one of his friends to ask if he would be going to Mumbai to watch the final, the friend not only refused to say anything, but even refused to let himself be photographed. His only comment was, "Yesterday some media people had come but I shooed them away."

Dhoni's elder brother Narendra Singh too refused to talk. He said if he talked about the match and his brother it would bring bad luck. He asked the reporter-photographer to come after the final, for sweets if India won.

On 2 April 2011, media personnel and fans camped in front

of his house for hours. Their vigil started much before the start of the final but they could not get even a glimpse of any member of the family. The house appeared deserted.

It was only after India had won the World Cup that his father and his mother made a brief appearance on one of the balconies and waved to the waiting fans. However, his parents and relatives and some close friends burst firecrackers to celebrate the victory. Those waiting outside heard the noise made by the crackers on the other side of the well guarded gate.

There was such a huge crowd of fans that traffic on the VIP road had come to a standstill. Many abandoned their idea of taking a drive past Dhoni's house just to have a look at his house. Some of those who could not control their curiosity, suffered. The fans, wild with frenzy, damaged many cars as they shattered windscreens and pulled out wipers and rear view mirrors.

A strong posse of policemen guarded the house. They resorted to laathi-charge to keep the excited fans at a distance. The situation would have turned very ugly but for the intervention by Gautam Gupta, and some friends.

However, his and his family's aversion to the media has made the life of the city based scribes that much more difficult. Reporters on the sports beat complain that whenever he comes home, the editor or the bureau chief wants exclusive reports. How does one get exclusive reports when no one from the family talks to the media?

Since March 2007, these so called exclusive reports have been confined to a few frames of MSD coming out of Ranchi airport, or a chance snap of Dhoni in his SUV at some place in the city.

And all the innumerable frames captured at Ranchi airport remain the same on all his visits. What distinguishes one frame from one of his visits to the next is the colour and design of his T-shirt and the position of the security personnel and his brother-in-law Gautam Gupta while escorting him to one of his SUVs.

***

7 Dhoni's Wedding

On 3 July 2010, Dhoni got engaged to Sakshi at Dehradun. The very next day they tied the knot. And, like many of his decisions on the cricket field, his marriage too took almost everyone by surprise; except his family members.

On 4 July 2010, three days before his 29th birthday, he tied the knot with Sakshi Singh Rawat, to put an end to all speculations: whether this most eligible bachelor was dating film actress Deepika Padukone, whether he was smitten by a certain Lakshmi, an Asin, or was there a secret girl in his life?

That day also ended the dream of thousands of girls, like Shiuli. She had followed him and managed to hug and kiss him, breaking the security cordon, on 6 May 2007 in Kolkata, when he was returning to the hotel from the conditioning camp, before India's tour of Bangladesh.

When he had gone to Bhopal for an ad shoot, a girl had run after his car. The media there got a sensational story.

The secret girl in his life turned out to be Sakshi Singh Rawat. Chased by females fans across the country, MSD finally settled for a girl whom his parents would have approved of without any hesitation. She belongs to the same caste, community and the state. Both are Kumaonis.

The wedding was solemnized at Vishranti, a resort in Dehradun, which again was so well fortified by the police and security personnel that no one from the media could get inside. They were kept at a healthy distance from the venue. When some of the media managed to accost some guest or relative, the response revealed nothing about the wedding schedule.

But the news channels, and the newspapers, including those in his home city, went ahead with whatever they could get or guess. This led to stories like the marriage being a culmination of their affair that started while both were students of Jawahar Vidya Mandir, Shyamali school.

Unaware of the difference of age between them, they also back calculated and put them together in the same batch. Some reported that Sakshi was a student of the Commerce stream.

Some local newspapers, claiming proximity to MSD, even reported that Sakshi's father was executive at MECON, and used to meet Dhoni's family frequently.

It turned out that Sakshi's father is an executive with a tea company and has been living in Alipore area in Calcutta for years. In the absence of any details forthcoming from the family, the media reporting became tales of fiction, which were hilarious, and to some extent irritating too. Even those local media personnel who claim to be close to MSD were stumped, literally.

They got the facts related to the bride and the wedding wrong and they stumbled again when on 7 July 2010, Dhoni came to his home city with his bride. That was his birthday too.

The media camped at the airport. But they could not get a byte from either Mr or Mrs Dhoni, or a frame of the couple at the airport.

Dhoni outplayed the media smartly. His SUV was parked at the exit of the airport. Luggage was loaded. His brother-in-law Gautam and friends hovered around the SUV. That convinced the media that they were waiting at the right spot. But Dhoni and his bride did not come out. Had they come out through the exit door that would have made an excellent visual.

While the camera men and reporters concentrated on the SUV, Dhoni and Sakshi were whisked away by a CISF officer through the gate at the other end. By the time the media could react, the couple had escaped. However, the persistent reporters rushed to his home, where hundreds of fans were already waiting for a glimpse of Dhoni and his bride. Fortunately, this chase ended on a satisfactory note as the couple appeared on the balcony for a brief while to acknowledge the greetings and obliged the media with a good frame.

At Dehradun too the media were kept at a distance, both before and during the engagement ceremony on 3 July and the wedding the next day. Expectedly, the media went overboard in running stories based on anticipation and hearsay.

One news channel kept showing a horse, moving in a semi-circle right through the day, 3 July, claiming that, that was the horse that MSD would ride to his wedding.

It must have amused MSD and members of his family to see so much fiction being paraded as facts related to his wedding.

Back home for a few days in November 2010, MSD spent some time with Jharkhand Jaguars at their Dhurwa camp. As the media were barred, a press photographer, waiting outside, overheard him telling the jawans about his favourite singers and songs. During that interaction, one of the jawans asked him about his avoiding the media. He was heard telling the jawans that he quite enjoyed playing hide and seek with the media.

It was revealed later, after the wedding, that two years ago MSD had met Sakshi at a 5-Star hotel in Calcutta, where she was doing internship as a student of hotel management. They met frequently thereafter.

However, despite all efforts at maintaining secrecy, way back in May, 2008, one Hindi newspaper had reported, one of Dhoni's meetings with Sakshi in Aurangabad.

MSD had made a quiet trip to Aurangabad in May 2008 while the Indian Premier League was in progress. He had put up at Rama International, a 5-Star hotel. From there he hired an auto and picked up Sakshi and her friend from the hotel management institute. They, then went to a lesser known restaurant. After dropping Sakshi and her friend back at the institute he returned to his hotel and immediately left for the airport.

On the return journey after dropping Sakshi, the auto driver told him he resembled Dhoni, captain of Team India. He said he wanted to confirm if he was really ferrying Dhoni, because if he was, he would treasure that brief meeting forever. Dhoni confirmed he was Dhoni.

After dropping him the auto driver was sharing his extraordinary experience with fellow drivers that his last passenger was no ordinary person but Team India's captain Dhoni. News spread fast but by the time the media could reach Hotel Rama International, he had left for the airport.

Later too there were reports that Dhoni was seen in Dehradun with Rudra Pratap Singh, his friend and India's fast bowler.

Despite such stray reports, for two years his friendship with Sakshi was a well kept secret. Even in his home city, where his close friends live, no one got even a whiff of this affair.

His engagement and wedding the following day might have appeared one of those sudden and surprise decisions a la Dhoni. But as actor Bipasha Basu, (one of his two close friends in Bollywood, the other being John Abraham), revealed to the media that the wedding was being planned for a long time. Some of his close friends knew of it fifteen days ahead of the wedding.

Later it also came to be known that preparations at Vishranti, had started fifteen days ahead of 4 July, the day he tied the nuptial ties with Sakshi in a traditional Kumaoni wedding. Here too no one, including the Dehradun based tent house owner who made arrangements, came to know that Vishranti was going to host Team India captain Dhoni's wedding.

But Ranchi, his home city, did come to play an important role. Some solace that! Their marriage was formally registered at Ranchi on 27 November. Treating this as a special case, the local authorities expedited the process of registration of their marriage, which is necessary these days for passport and visa. This hasty registration of their marriage must have made it easier for Sakshi to accompany him on his tours abroad.

However, for the wedding ceremony at Dehradun, the select guest list included cine star John Abraham, cricketer RP Singh and Suresh Raina and Sudesh Mahto, Jharkhand sports minister. From his home city he invited Santosh Lal, Gautam Upadhaya, and Paramjit Singh. Of course, his parents, elder brother and his wife, and sister Jayanti and brother-in-law Gautam Gupta with their parents were there.

Later, in November, John Abraham told a news channel that at Dhoni's wedding he had danced to his heart's content. He really enjoyed being there as very few guests attended the ceremony.

Interestingly, on 4 July 2010, while MSD should have been getting ready for the wedding ceremony at Dehradun, the BCCI president Shashank Manohar and secretary N Srinivasan were in Ranchi. They had flown to the city to attend the inauguration of the indoor cricket facility at the under construction international stadium of Jharkhand State Cricket Stadium.

The BCCI president Manohar and the BCCI secretary Srinivasan, who is also the owner of Chennai Super Kings in Indian Premier League, said they wanted to see Dhoni's home city. Srinivasan was more keen to do so because under him Chennai Super Kings had won IPL III.

Naturally, the media were eager to know if the BCCI president Shashank Manohar was going to Dehradun to attend Dhoni's wedding. Manohar quipped, "*Jaane ka sawal to tab uthoga jab nimantran ho*" (the question of going for the wedding arises if there is an invitation). Manohar and Srinivasan flew back to Mumbai in the afternoon.

The select guest list comprised a dozen persons. The likes of the BCCI president and the secretary too did not belong to that select list.

This should be balm to the hurt egos of many, who had played cricket with him and who thought they were close to him. All the speculations regarding the wedding reception whether it would be at Ranchi, or at Mumbai, remained mere speculations. No function was held at Ranchi.

This just shows how private a person MSD is, and how much he treasurers his privacy.

***

8
Dhoni's Family

MSD carries the values given by his parents. Among other things, a person with good values is one who is respectful to his elders, does not have vices and is courteous and disciplined. MSD has imbibed these qualities from his parents. That is why everyone talks about how grounded and down to earth he remains, despite reaching such dizzy heights.

Pan Singh, his father, is a Khas Rajput from Lwali village in Almora district in Uttarakhand. He does not use the family surname "Dhoni", which in the native dialect is "*Dhauni*". Though belonging to an agricultural family, Pan Singh decided to get a job. The search for a job took him to Bokaro Steel City, via Lucknow, where the Bokaro Steel Plant was coming up. By the time he reached Bokaro all the vacancies were filled up.

In 1964, he got a job at Hindustan Steel Limited, which later became Metallurgical and Engineering Consultants (MECON). He was one of the staff deputed to look after water supply to

Shyamali Colony. Five years later Devaki joined him. The couple have three children–Narendra, Jayanti and Mahendra.

The family has remained in touch with their native village and members of their family, like uncles and aunts, who still live there. Dhoni's sacred thread ceremony was performed there eight years ago. The village priest is still consulted frequently on auspicious occasions.

As mentioned elsewhere, Pan Singh's commitment to maintain a regular supply of water to the Mecon stadium, where turf wickets and the outfield were being prepared for hosting a Ranji match, even in the face of water rationing and the post Indira Gandhi assasintation in 1984, is still remembered.

When Dhoni had become a super star and the small one-bed room flat at Shyamali Colony made it difficult to host visitors, Pan Singh, took out his bicycle and pedalled down to Mecon office to request for a more spacious accommodation. Then chairman-cum-managing director Drona Rath, a former Mecon cricket player himself, readily allotted a spacious bungalow meant for senior executives.

Then, at the time of Jharkhand Assembly elections, the media were amazed to see Pan Singh, standing in a queue, waiting for his turn to cast his vote. He continues to be the way he was before his youngest child became a super star.

Dhoni's mother, Devaki Devi, while the family lived in Mecon's Shyamali colony, used to go on a rickshaw for buying vegetables and grocery items.

Significantly, by this time Dhoni had a few SUVs and cars, including one Mitsubishi Pajero, one Scorpio and one Toyota

Corolla. But his parents have continued their old life style, though their life now is constantly under the media glare.

A man of few words, Pan Singh still continues to be a humble person. These days he has to attend several functions as stand-by for his son MSD. Be it the inauguration of the indoor cricket facility at the under construction international cricket stadium of JSCA, or some programme organized to felicitate MSD, Pan Singh has to be invited as a stand in for his son, who is usually not available for such functions. Though he attends all such functions, dressed in plain shirt and trousers, and a cap on his head, he hardly speaks. Until summoned to take his chair on the dais he keeps himself in the background.

He is a stickler for discipline in the family. MSD admitted in an interview, "My father is a strict disciplinarian," and that he was more free with his mother, Devaki Devi and elder sister Jayanti.

Pan Singh calling out "*Mahiya*" used to make him leave anything he was doing. But later, as Dhoni started getting recognition in cricket, he accepted that his youngest son was on the right track.

The turning point in the father-son relationship vis-à-vis studies versus games perhaps came after Dhoni scored those 213 runs in the inter-school cricket final and he was signed up by Central Coalfields Limited at a healthy stipend of Rs 2200 per month.

MSD is invariably called Maahi, though it should be Mahi, 'a' being a schwa as the one in "about". His father had told this writer, soon after Dhoni's first tour to Bangladesh in December 2004, "Don't know why they call him Maahi, he is Mahi." At home, however, he calls him *Mahiya.*

Pan Singh, a keen football player himself, wanted his "*Mahiya*" to concentrate more on studies. As an employee of a public sector undertaking, with a low position because of lack of education, he understood the value of education. Fortunately, MSD went to one of the best schools in the city, DAV Shyamali, which was maintained by the MECON management.

Like most doting mothers, Devaki Devi supported her youngest child and she continues to so. In February 2011 she went to Dhoni's native village for a nephew's marriage. On her return journey, she had to stop at Haldwani, the nearest railway station from Lwali, their native village. She made sure she carried back to Ranchi some CDs of MSD's favourite Kumaoni songs, "*O Chandu driver, gaari mithoo mithoo chala re...,*" as well as ingredients for preparing his favourite Kumaoni dishes.

And what was the mode of transport that Pan Singh and Devaki Devi used at Haldwani for calling on relatives and for shopping? They used rickshaws and autorickshaws. They could have hired an air conditioned taxi, but didn't.

His sister Jayanti, elder to him, dotes on him. It was sweet and thoughtful of her to gift him a diamond pendant, displaying the number seven, MSD's lucky number and the date of his birth too, on his twenty-fifth birthday in 2006.

A good student, Jayanti helped her brother brush up topics for examinations. She was his anchor and perhaps his good luck charm too. Dhoni said in an interview that he was closer to his sister than his elder brother Narendra.

In class X he scored 66 per cent, and in class XII he got 56 per cent 1999. His studies did suffer as he had started playing for teams like CCL and the under-19 state level tournaments. MSD himself, once confessed in an interview, that he loved playing more than studying.

When he started touring as a member of Team India, on his return home he would first go to Jayanti's home in North Office Para. After meeting her and leaving his kit bag at her place would he head for his home. When leaving home for a tour or tournament, he would meet Jayanti, collect his kit bag and head directly to the airport. Sources close to the family say that had become a ritual, and apparently Dhoni considered this auspicious. She is now a teacher at Jawahar Vidya Mandir, Shyamali, where she, her husband and Dhoni too had studied.

"Jayanti, who teachers in the primary section, Class III to V, continues to be a down-to-earth lady, without a touch of arrogance. She comes to school on a scooty, and not in an expensive vehicle. Her behaviour does not betray that she is the sister of Mahendra Singh Dhoni," says Keshav Ranjan Banerjee, sports teacher at the school.

Professor Jayant Sinha of ST Xavier's College, who interacted with Dhoni and Jayanti at the time of admitting him in the college for BCom Honours, also found Jayanti, "without a touch of arrogance, and very down to earth."

Some of his motorcycles and vehicles, gifted to him for his match winning performances, occupy the parking space where Jayanti lives with her in-laws, the Guptas, in the multi-storey complex at North Office Para

MSD's brother-in-law Gautam, though two years his senior

at school, has been his constant companion since his school days. Once an aspiring cricket player, Gautam formed a local club and started participating in tournaments held in and around Ranchi. Naturally, Dhoni was one of the important players in that team. Gautam took it upon himself to guide his more talented friend, Mahi. Besides taking him from one ground to the other on his scooter, or arranging kit and other facilities, he was like his cricketing shadow. Those close to Dhoni and Gautam also say that Dhoni's love for computer games was another hobby that they shared.

Even today, he continues to be constantly by his side when Dhoni is in his home city. If Gautam is in the city, it is taken for granted that he would be there to receive and see off MSD at the airport. His presence at the airport is taken for granted so much so that once when he was in Calcutta in connection with his business, Dhoni's elder brother Narendra went to receive him. That became news for the local media. Some reported that for the first time his elder brother had gone to receive him. And some, who may not have been at the airport and did not care to cross check, reported that Dhoni's brother and his brother-in-law were there to receive him at the airport!

His elder brother, Narendra, too, used to be a football player. The eldest among the three siblings, he had gone back to their native village. But he returned after his younger brother's successes on the cricket field and in endorsements. After a brief flirtation with politics at the local level, when he sat on some dharnas for local issues, he now looks after distributorship of a mobile phone.

He has some very close friends too, with whom he relaxes whenever he is in Ranchi.

These are Santosh Lal, Gautam Upadhyaya, Simant Lohani and Paramjit Singh. Of these Santosh Lal is a Ranji player and has been his team mate at the CCL too. These are the friends who accompany him to dhabas and the Deori temple. These are the friends with whom he watches cricket matches on television when at home.

Incidentally, MSD's sister Jayanti, brother-in-law Gautam Gupta and friend Gautam Upadhaya, were in the same school, and college.

Among his friends, Paramjit deserves a special mention. He persuaded a bat making company to sponsor Dhoni's kit when he was yet to make his mark at the higher level. Those who know of their friendship still remember the season when Dhoni broke as many as eight bats, and Paramjit kept replacing the broken bats. Those days he could not have afforded to buy so many bats in one season. Such support perhaps helped him play his uninhibited brand of cricket.

That is the small and intimate circle around MSD. Of course, now his wife Sakshi is also a part of it.

***

9
Dhoni Overcomes Cricketing Handicaps

His emergence as an international cricket player from the so called backwaters of cricket in the country and his meteoric rise to the most coveted position in Indian cricket, that of the captain of Team India, has made MSD a national icon.

He is seen as an icon of what a strong self belief, a strong will and a single minded pursuit of one's chosen goal, can achieve.

But few are aware of the handicaps that he had to overcome to get where he is today.

He has kindled hope in many hearts–young cricketers and their parents, that it is possible to rise from a humble background and become a prosperous cricketer. All the coaching centres in the city recorded a sudden increase in the number of trainees. These days it is a common sight to see aspiring young cricketers, carrying hefty kit bags, come to a coaching centre, with very young ones accompanied by one of the parents.

However, a brief look at the handicaps that he faced when he switched over from canvas ball cricket to proper cricket in 1994-95 makes his achievements all the more remarkable; verging on the miraculous, one might say.

Would anyone readily believe that in those days there was only one turf wicket, with grass covered outfield in the city where Dhoni was born and where he learnt his cricket? That was at the Mecon stadium. Debal Sahay, a former cricketer and general manager at Mecon had persuaded Bihar Cricket Association, (Bihar was not bifurcated then) to allot a Ranji match to Ranchi. The Mecon management agreed to prepare a turf wicket at its stadium.

About a decade later, the second turf wicket, courtesy Central Mine Planning and Design Institute, a Coal India Limited subsidiary company, was constructed at Birsa Munda stadium at Morabadi in 1994, for that season's Wills Trophy match between Bombay and Wills XI. Debal Sahay had moved to CMPDI as a chief general manager, and was in charge of sports.

That wicket was also used for two super league matches of Ranji Trophy and one Deodhar Trophy match between the East Zone and Central Zone.

But as it happens in small cricket centres, that wicket was damaged when that stadium hosted a musical night, featuring Asha Bhonsle and other cine stars. Cricket fans were aghast that holes were dug right across the field, including the pitch, for that show.

Thus, when Dhoni started playing serious cricket there was only one turf wicket in his city.

Hence, MSD took the correct cricketing decision in 1998 to move to the Central Coalfields Limited team, where they had a turf wicket for practice.

However, in his formative years, Dhoni played most of his matches on matting wickets, which of course made him a powerful backfoot player, whose staple shots were cuts, hooks and pulls. In hindsight this may have helped in hooking Pakistan speedster Shoaib Akhtar to signal domination from the word go.

Besides that, some of these matting wickets were choir mats spread over hard and plain part of a rock hard ground. Often the pitch would be a 22-yard strip on a hard ground that was smoothened by rubbing the surface with a few bricks. The mat, more often than not would be in a worn out condition, especially around the popping crease where bowlers' front foot, with boots with spikes, landed while delivering a ball. Those worn out patches, sometimes covered with a piece of tarpaulin, affected a batsman's footwork. If left uncovered the feet got stuck, if covered they would slip. But that was how matches were played.

It was in such conditions on a matting wicket that February day in 1997, that he scored those 213 runs in that inter-school final played at Harmu ground.

The outfield of the grounds that he played on namely Harmu, Archery, Ranchi College and others were rock hard surfaces devoid of grass. Even for a wicketkeeper, it was an injury inviting exercise to dive and stop a ball and a new cricket ball would get scuffed within a few overs. Thus, the ball could swing for very few overs, which deprived the batsmen of practice against swinging balls. This technical deficiency ended some potential careers.

Those were the playing conditions that MSD had to bear with in his formative years.

The inter-district cricket tournaments at all levels were played in vastly differing playing conditions. If the pitches and over all playing conditions were good at most of the grounds in Jamshedpur, that was because the steel city was the headquarters of cricket in this state, and the Tatas played an active role in promoting sports. That is why, players of this city, were better placed than their peers from other cities.

Besides playing conditions they had the advantage of playing with senior Ranji players in local tournaments. Add to that a number of coaching schools with experienced Ranji players, past and present, readily available for guidance. Thus, young players of the steel city started with a distinct advantage over their peers from the districts. In contrast, the facilities at district headquarters used to be dismal.

MSD and the Ranchi district school players will never forget what they went through at Giridih during the inter-district school tournament. Their accommodation was so poor that before leaving for the ground, the players had to perform their morning ablutions outdoors. 'Four or five of us carried water in empty cold drink bottles and were mortified when pigs charged at us,' recalls Raunak Dhari Singh, teammate of MSD at Jawahar Vidya Mandir School, Shyamali. Credit should be given to the boys who retained their enthusiasm and continued to play. MSD was one of them.

As majority of the district cricket associations were not financially strong, teams were put up in some dharmshala or a cheap hotel. Usually, all the 15 players had to stay in one big hall. Mosquito repellents were an essential item of a player's kit.

Despite such conditions, a district cricket association office bearer says, MSD, who had just crossed the 19-year mark, accompanied a district Under-19 team to Gumla. Though he was not a member of the team, as he was over 19 then, he stayed with the team amidst such conditions. "That showed his commitment to the game and the team. He did not mind those trying conditions as he wanted to be with the team," the official said.

Ground conditions too were far from ideal at such centres. Sight screens were a rarity. Comforts of a pavilion were unheard of. Tents and some plastic chairs were considered a privilege. "Such dismal conditions do affect a player's performance," Adil Hussain agrees.

Thus a player, aiming high, had to be mentally tough to sustain his interest and enthusiasm for the game. MSD, of course, had these qualities in plenty to have graduated through these stages to higher grades to become number one in the ICC rankings. And to emerge as one of the most successful captains, with two World Cup titles.

***

10
Dhoni Shows His Mettle Early

Today everyone hails MSD for his ability to take decisions, and stand by those decisions; be it selection of a player, or a toss, or handing over the ball to the least expected bowler in moments of crisis.

He may have been a raw 17-year old but even in those early days he took some decisive steps, like his decision to move to CCL cricket team, leaving behind the Steel Authority of India's corporate unit, Research and Development Centre for Iron and Steel team, which was paying him a stipend too.

From 1998 to 2002, he played for the public sector undertaking CCL. Why did he choose to play for CCL, over and above the others?

The answer to that reveals how clear he was in his mind, even in those early days, what he needed to do to rise in cricket.

He preferred CCL for its practice facilities. He had played for R&D for one season but he was not satisfied with the amount of practice he got there. In the Railways team he was asked to bat lower down. As far as Mecon was concerned, he did not even turn up for selection trials because he did not like the comment, made by a former Ranji player and one of the Mecon selectors, 'he does not know how to bat and he does not possess technique required of a good batsman'.

This decision paid rich dividends. He was guided by Debal Sahay, who as director (personnel) had taken the initiative to form the cricket team.

As first class and big matches are played on turf wickets, it was a good move as CCL headquarters at Darbhanga House had a turf wicket for practice.

Debal Sahay saw to it that the turf wicket was prepared even before the team was put together. MSD was the first player to be signed. He got Rs 2200 as monthly stipend, the highest amount among stipend players, including some Ranji players.

In addition to kits and stipend, he was entitled to travelling and daily allowances too, whenever the team participated in tournaments away from the headquarters. What more could an aspiring cricketer have asked for in those days?

Besides that, practice facilities at CCl were just ideal for grooming a talented and committed player like Dhoni. "We used to provide two new balls for each session at the nets, which helped the top order batsmen to bat against a new ball against good fast bowlers. As Dhoni batted second in the nets, he got to play against fast bowlers who were already playing Ranji matches. This must have boosted his confidence and honed his skills, 'says Adil Hussain, a former Ranji batsman and captain of the CCL team.

For the team too MSD's inclusion turned out to be a good decision. He, singlehandedly through his batting, took the CCL team from B Division to A Division in the local league tournament conducted by Ranchi District Cricket Association.

Later, he went on to play many more match winning knocks for them in tournaments across the country, like Inter-Coal, or Sheesh Mahal, and others in places like Nagpur, Lucknow, Dehradun and in Orissa and Chhatisgarh.

"The CCL team played 40 to 50 matches every season. In tournaments like Sheesh Mahal summer cricket, we played against teams which fielded, then current India players like fast bowler Debashish Mohanty, and for a young player like Dhoni to have scored runs against them must have boosted his confidence to a new level," says Adil Hussain.

The team not only participated in many tournaments across the country, but took its practice sessions seriously. When not playing in tournaments, the team used to practise for three to four hours every day, from 6.30 am to 10.30 am.

Once the team was travelling to Brajraj Nagar in Orissa. The team had left by train, but four or five players were travelling by a Sumo, along with their director. MSD offered to travel in the luggage boot as there was a space crunch. He travelled lying or sleeping over the kit bags. The distance covered was around 350 km. That's a hardy, uncomplaining and undemanding boy for you!

His team mates recall another incident from a tournament in Orissa in 2002-03. The match was being played on a matting wicket. A fast ball reared up and broke his left wrist. He got the wrist bandaged and opted to bowl as he couldn't have kept wickets with a broken wrist. He put in a spell of fiery bowling, capturing three wickets. His team mates knew he could bowl fast but what amazed them was his spirit. Despite that injury he did not want to stay behind in the pavilion. "Any other player would have thought of his injury and played safe, but this boy, a perfect team member and a committed player took the field, and contributed to his team's success," remembers Debal Sahay.

Earlier, in 2000-2001, at a tournament in Lucknow, the CCL team was playing against the home team. Batting second, Lucknow were cruising along and defeat was staring the CCL team in its face. "When five or seven overs remained, I asked Dhoni to take off his pads, and bowl. He bowled so well that besides checking the flow of runs, he also took some wickets and pressure on the batting side kept mounting. We won that match, and went on to win the tournament," recalls Adil Hussain.

Then, at the nets at the CCL headquarters, players would hold a competition among themselves as to who would clear the tall eucalyptus trees at the far end of the practice ground. A batsman would get a treat of tea and '*aloo tikkis*' if he would clear the tallest tree at the far end of the practice ground. The bowlers too would bowl seriously to avoid being hit for a six. "It was tough competition between bat and ball," recalls Hussain.

Needless to mention, Dhoni won those bets frequently and enjoyed the treat at the end of practice sessions. Who knew then that the boy hitting those huge lofted shots would go on to wow the cricketing world with his power shots?

As, at CCL they used to have regular and long practice

Krishnamachari Srikkanth said, "He is very street smart, has got a strong head, has belief in his players, let his players do their job, don't interfere."

Former captain and legendary leg spinner Anil Kumble said, "He is very calm and non-emotional."

As an expert on a news channel, Ajay Jadeja, with a twinkle in his eyes, quipped, "If Sourav Ganguly is a "*Dada*" of a captain then Dhoni would be a "*Goonda*" of a captain. He must have meant that as a captain Dhoni was a street smart captain who was quick in countering moves made by the opposing captain.

To South Africa's wicketkeeper-batsman Mark Boucher, who has more than 500 dismissals in Test cricket and more than 400 dismissals in one day internationals, Dhoni is a bold captain who shuns the conservative approach in favour of innovative ideas.

Ravi Shastri, who reads the game well, makes an important point about his leadership qualities when he says that Dhoni has managed the egos in the dressing room so well. It is in the clash of egos that many captains lose their hold.

In managing egos in the dressing room Dhoni reminds us of Mike Brearley, former England captain, who managed volatile personalities like Ian Botham very well. He was known to be good at understanding the personalities of his team mates, and knew how to take the best out of each of his players. That is why, despite his poor form with the bat, the English selectors asked him to lead England on its tour of Australia in 1978-79. England retained the Ashes with 5-1 victory in Tests.

Dhoni's success in managing the egos is reflected in the way Sachin Tendulkar is performing these days, both in Tests and

ODIs. Sachin was not playing freely when Greg Chappel was the coach because the dressing room those days was not the happiest place to be in.

He must be an expert in man-management, too, because of the way he has handled senior players, all former captains too, like Sachin, Rahul Dravid and Sourav Ganguly, and volatile personalities like Yuvraj Singh, Harbhajan Singh and Sreesanth.

Yes, MSD has deserved the accolades showered on him for his captaincy.

As a captain he has also shown his mettle by remaining unperturbed and ignoring criticism. He has stood by his decisions, be it selection of a player, or changes in bowling or the batting order.

However, some former cricketers, including former captain and great left arm spinner Bishen Singh Bedi, even called him obstinate for persisting with Piyush Chawla and then for his faith in Ashish Nehra. Bedi must have feared such obstinacy might harm Team India's interests.

But MSD remained unfazed. He remained committed to his decisions, to his strategy, and got the results that he and every one craved for: winning the World Cup.

Another facet of his personality that emerged is that even in the face of overwhelming pressure he has shown that he has the courage to admit his mistakes too.

After defeating Pakistan in the semi-final at Mohali on 30 March 2011, he was candid in admitting at the presentation ceremony: "I misread the pitch". Otherwise, he would have opted for a spin dominated bowling attack.

His candid admission that he had misread the pitch, that too after winning the match, prompted Imran Khan to describe that statement as "a bold captain's courageous statement."

Perhaps no other captain, in the euphoria of the victory over Pakistan would have felt the need to admit he had misread the pitch. Equally readily, he points out mistakes committed by others.

At the presentation ceremony after the World Cup final he said (with a smile of course), "Gautam Gambhir (97 runs) has to blame himself for getting out when he was just three runs away from his century."

After the presentation ceremony, he very smartly anticipated Ravi Shastri's queries. Before Shastri could ask him anything, he said, "Well of course, we needed to win because otherwise I would have to answer a few questions… why I included Sreesanth and not Ashwin, and why I came in to bat ahead of Yuvi…." With that statement he pre-empted questions that Shastri would have asked. He had also answered his detractors and some of the experts as well.

And who will forget those September 2007 nights in South Africa when India kept winning matches on way to winning the inaugural edition of the T20 World Cup.

Earlier, after winning the T20 semi-final against Australia, Dhoni stumped Ravi Shastri at the post-match presentation ceremony. He told Ravi Shastri, "We have proved you wrong." He was referring to Shastri's pre-match view published in newspapers that Australia were the favourites to win the semi-final. Dhoni had read that piece.

In fact, at most of the post-match presentation ceremonies, he candidly points out where the team went wrong, in batting, bowling or fielding. During the World Cup too, he admitted candidly that the Indian team's fielding was not up to the international standard. But he added, that this shortcoming had to be made up by scoring more runs and putting pressure on the opponents.

Way back in October 2008, Sachin Tendular had told an English news channel that he (Dhoni) had situational awareness. This could have been the reason that Sachin had recommended his name to lead India in the inaugural edition of the T20 World Cup, 2007, when the BCCI selectors were looking for a suitable captain as both Virendra Sehwag and Yuvraj Singh were in indifferent form. How satisfied Sachin must have felt when India won that Cup!

He was like that even in his earlier days, outspoken but polite. During his CCL days, in a tight match one medium fast bowler, Anshuman Raj asked his captain Adil Hussain, for the ball, with the confidence that he would do the job, that is win the match. The CCL team lost the match. Dhoni candidly, though politely told that senior player, "*Anshu Bhaiya, agli baar ball mat mangiyega* (Don't ask for the ball again)."

"He never minced his words at the team meetings and would always point out mistakes committed by others. But he was never rude or impolite while doing so," says Adil Hussain.

Maintaining his cool in adverse situations has been his forte in his early days in cricket too. Recalls Santosh Lal, his close friend and a Ranji player, "In a Ranji match against Kerala, the

Jharkhand batting collapsed. Dhoni walked in to bat at number five or seven but there was no trace of the tension that the team was in. He walked out, and batted freely, tore apart the Kerala attack, and bailed the team out."

He does not let an adverse situation unsettle him.

There was this inter-district final match against Dhanbad at Dhanbad. The defending champions, the Ranchi District team, was depleted because three of its top batsmen, all Ranji players, did not report for the match as they did not want to play under SB Choubey, the captain, who was junior to them. But MSD batted like a champion and scored undefeated 154 runs. Courtesy that knock, Ranchi's innings remained incomplete when the match ended, and the inter-district Hayman trophy was shared. To top it all, at the toss for deciding which team would keep the trophy for the first five months, Ranchi won the toss and the team returned home with the trophy.

To remain unruffled and approach a dicey situation on a cricket field with an open, uncluttered mind, continues to be his strength even in the international arena.

What does he expect from his team mates? As he himself said, after losing to New Zealand by five wickets at Wellington, in 2009, "I am not an angry captain. I am not too worried about the result. I am more concerned about the commitment and effort."

Therein lies the key to his success as a captain. He is more concerned about commitment and effort of players rather than the result.

***

12
Shaurya

"That's Dhoni's house." When relatives or friends come to this city, the host makes it a point to show them his house in Harmu Housing Colony.

His official home address is: SHAURYA H A10. Add to this Harmu Housing Colony, Ranchi, and you have the complete postal address.

The name of the house befits the character and career of Mahi; in Hindi it means bravery.

This new tourist destination, if one might say so, is ideally located. It stands next to the State Bank of India, Harmu branch, on the VIP road which takes ministers and officials to the Project Building, Jharkhand's administrative headquarters. The Bhartiya Janta Party's state headquarters, on the other side of the road is nearby. A new petrol pump has been opened right across the road. Perhaps their chief customer in the days to come would be Dhoni with his fleet of five cars and 22 motorcycles.

Architecturally, this house stands out.

A look at it confirms the saying that a house is a reflection of its owner's personality. Dhoni's house is just that. Rectangular blocks symmetrically arranged give it an air of solidity.

But this dream house, the owner's pride, attracted some envy from its neighbours. While it was under construction, some neighbours filed complaints with Ranchi Regional Development Authority. They asked for recall of permission to build a swimming pool, alleging that it would consume four lakh gallons of water. Where would the used water from the swimming pool go? Can a residential colony, plagued with water shortage, afford such huge consumption by one house alone?

This matter was taken to the court. Seventeen neighbours, including some retired police officials, had signed the petition to RRDA.

As it turned out, the L-shaped swimming pool, was meticulously planned. It was designed by a Calcutta based architect.

The use of the latest technology would ensure that water would be re-cycled and recharge pit without drains would prevent water from being released on the colony roads. Besides, as the swimming pool, 150ft × 40ft × 10ft, would be filled up with water coming from a borewell, it would not be using water from the regular supply system.

However, the petition was disallowed in the court and RRDA too, did not withdraw its sanction.

It comes as no surprise therefore that the members of the Dhoni family hardly interact with their neighbours. This house is built on a 5000 square feet plot, of which 4500 square feet was gifted by the state government, led by chief minister Arjun Munda in 2006 after MSD's triumphant tour of Pakistan.

However, as the original plot was found to be a bit inadequate for his dream house, Dhoni sought special permission to purchase the adjoining piece of land from the state housing board.

It is a self-sufficient unit, with a transformer. Sources say rooms and bathrooms are equipped with imported tiles and gadgets. There is facility for gymnasium and indoor practice; everything one can think of is there.

The rectangular plot has got huge gates, in the front and the rear as well. If Dhoni wants to hoodwink his fans standing in front of the building, he can easily drive away through the rear gate. Or, he can drive in through the main entrance and can continue to drive on and exit at the other end. Though this house has roads on three sides, (the State Bank of India branch occupies the 4th side) privacy is well protected.

Dhoni, despite his busy cricketing and endorsement schedules, closely followed the construction of this house. On every visit home, he inspected the construction site, and sources say he chose the colours, tiles, and the gadgets personally.

It is well fortified, which was to be expected given the popularity that he enjoys. Security guards, both private and police, man the entrance round the clock. Closed circuit television cameras assist the security personnel. Besides protecting the property, their main brief is to keep uninvited guests on the other side of the main gate.

Yet one of the CCTVs installed at the rear of the house was stolen when the family were away for a few days in February

2011. The mysterious theft remains unsolved.

However, fans need to be grateful that Dhoni has provided for a balcony that faces the main entrance of the house on the VIP road.

It is on this balcony that on 7 July 2010, his 29th birthday and three days after his wedding, Mr and Mrs MS Dhoni made a brief appearance to acknowledge greetings from hundreds of fans who had gathered for a glimpse of their newly-wed hero. After hours of waiting, they got a glimpse of the couple for a few minutes. They cheered and went back happy.

On 2 April 2011, the night after the World Cup final, Shaurya was the destination for thousands of fans. Though they knew Dhoni was in Mumbai, they gathered outside his home, demanding a "*darshan*" of his parents. The VIP road was choked. Many families, curious to see what was going on at his home, were stranded. The local police had a tough time controlling the fans who even attempted to break the security cordon and scale the wall.

Yes, that house is so well known that if someone drops a card with only MS Dhoni, Ranchi written in the address column, it would reach its destination.

***

13 Dhoni's Heart Reaches Out to the Underprivileged

She is twenty years old; she earns around Rs 4,500 a month and is the only breadwinner in her family. This Ranchi lady was devastated when she found she had a hole in her heart, a congenital heart condition that required surgery. She was not in a position to afford the surgery, which normally costs a few lakh rupees.

The Rotary India Heart Foundation (RIHF) came to her rescue and as her case had the reference of Mahendra Singh Dhoni, the RIHF brand ambassador, her case was taken up on a priority basis. She walked out of the Durgapur health centre of RIHF with a healthy and normal heart.

Hers and her family's blessings would always be with Dhoni. Her name has been deliberately withheld keeping in mind her future, when she would like to have a family and set up her own home.

The Rotarians were apprehensive that he, Dhoni, being such

a busy man, with the World Cup matches and his endorsements, it would be difficult to get in touch with him and get his consent for becoming the brand ambassador for "Join Me in Saving Little Hearts" campaign of Rotary India Heart Foundation.

But when this proposal reached him, via Dr Harsh Dev Sharan, a close family friend, he readily agreed.

This campaign was launched to help poor children, who are suffering from congenital heart problems requiring surgery, and whose families cannot afford the life saving surgery. The Foundation has targeted to help 2000 such children of the SAARC countries over three years.

RIHF, founded in 2010, was looking for a brand ambassador whose association with this cause would help generate funds. Each surgery costs minimum of Rs 60,000, and if a case is complicated the cost may go up to Rs 2.5 lakh. The Rotary Club that refers a child for such treatment pays Rs 20,000 as sponsorship amount. Nothing is to be charged from the child's family.

The surgeon, chosen to perform the surgery, donates his expertise and charges nothing.

Says Sharan, "When the request reached him he was in South Africa. On his return he asked Gautam, his brother-in-law, to get in touch with me to confirm his commitment to this cause and ask what else needed to be done."

The campaign slogan — Save Little Hearts — and the poster featuring MSD were sent to him for approval.

At the RIHF foundation day function at Calcutta on 23 February 2010, the poster with MSD's photograph and the appeal, "Join Me in Saving Little Hearts," was unveiled. All the

Rotarians stood up in the hall to applaud their brand ambassador. "The spontaneous standing ovation was overwhelming and I felt very proud that our Mahi has become so popular even among the older generation," says Sharan.

Back in his home city, his friends and relatives visit the children of Michael Blind School on special occasions and distribute fruits, sweets and gifts among them. The last such special occasion came when India won the World Cup, 2011.

On his birthday in 2010, those visually challenged children composed a song for their cricketing idol and benefactor.

In March 2008, on one of his visits, he played an exhibition football match at Silli Sports Academy, at Silli.

The day after the match he gifted Reebok shoes to thirty football players of the Academy. The cost came to around rupees one and a half lakh. The amount may be insignificant keeping his financial profile, but what is commendable is the spirit behind this gesture.

Being a keen football player himself, before he took to cricket, he must have felt the talented young players needed encouragement and support.

And who would know better than him the value of quality equipment for a sportsman!

The same sentiment was behind the district level T20 cricket tournament that was organized by Mahendra Singh Dhoni Charitable Trust. It was launched by him in February 2011 at the Jharkhand State Cricket Association's international cricket stadium in Ranchi. The purpose behind it was to select talented young players, who are underprivileged, and provide financial assistance to send one of them to a coaching academy in Australia. Dhoni took a day out of his busy schedule and flew in to inaugurate this tournament on 4 February 2011.

Similar sentiments must have made him send his wife Sakshi in November 2010, with winter setting in, to distribute blankets among the rural poor in a village near Ranchi.

Earlier, he agreed to be a part of the government of Jharkhand's campaign – '*Aao School Chale*'. He did a shoot which shows him asking children to come to school because education is very important. That message was reinforced when it was widely reported that Dhoni had enrolled at St Xavier's College for graduation in the commerce stream.

***

14
Dhoni Reveals Dhoni

MSD is a charismatic cricketer. Hugely successful, both in terms of performance on the cricket field and in piling up one endorsement after another.

But he has not allowed success to go to his head. It has not made him vain, egotistic or complacent. He continues to be genial, humble and tolerant.

What would be a better way to get a glimpse into his mind than to study his own words, spoken on different occasions, at different points of time.

A month after his career defining knock of 148 runs against Pakistan at Visakhapatnam, 5 April 2005, he told a newspaper, "It's all come overnight. The cameras used to pass me by; now they are stopping for me." This statement shows he is aware of the nature of the glamour factor that comes with success.

On another occasion, he cleared the myth that he drinks four litres of milk a day. "Ravi Shastri said that in a post match presentation, at Vishakhapatnam, but I don't consume four litres of milk in a day; it's closer to around one litre of buffalo milk. Now I've shifted to milk shakes, but I ensure that I get my daily quota."

MSD said, elsewhere, that he did love milk when he was a child, was fond of fruits and, was a vegetarian. Mango shake continues to be his favourite drink.

On the cricket field he remains cool but that does not mean that he does not get angry.

He lost his cool at Nottingham when he perceived a reporter was suggesting that it was Dhoni who had leaked the news about Virendra Sehwag's fitness to a particular reporter. He does lose his cool but he also knows he should tame his anger.

He explains why he remains cool instead of giving vent to his anger. "There are times when it is really difficult to control yourself, but you have to. Because it's cricket, not boxing." This also explains why he has never been involved in an ugly exchange of words or a brawl on the cricket field.

In another interview he told a newspaper, "I am what I am. It's not that I am always calm and composed. But... I don't believe that losing your mind is the right way to go ahead."

He can be sarcastic too. Perhaps he uses sarcasm as a weapon to conceal his anger and yet release the steam. Like it happened on 25 October 2007, after India had won the inaugural edition of T20 World Cup. He was being felicitated by the then chief minister of Jharkhand, Madhu Koda, at his official residence. That provided a rare occasion for the local media to ask him a few questions because he had been shunning them since the orchestrated protests, earlier that year after the exit of India from the World Cup, 2007. When some one asked him about his girl friend, he quipped, "Thank you for changing my girlfriend every now and then."

Indeed, when asked by an English news channel to describe himself, he had said, "I can be sarcastic." When he gets angry with someone, he uses sarcasm instead of shouting at him. One example comes readily to mind; when the stump mike caught him telling a fielder, who was just that bit slow in running after the ball in a match in Australia in 2008, "*match ke baad sone ke liye kaafi waqt milega*" (You will get plenty of time to sleep after the match).

Sarcasm is also evident in his take on pressure. To a national fortnightly he said, "There is pressure if you win, pressure if you lose." And then he qualified it with, "I would have told you the exact figure (of pressure, of course) if I had a machine to measure it."

Everyone who has followed his career knows he handles pressure better than most, particularly better than his predecessors. Ravi Shastri remarked, "Dhoni's USP is that he never loses composure, doesn't allow his body language to give anything away." In the tensest of situations, all you can see on his face while he is standing behind the stumps, is an expression that betrays nothing. Jog your memory a bit and compare that with changes in facial expression of even an aggressive captain like Sourav Ganguly. His face always betrayed what he was feeling during tense moments in a match.

At times he turns a philosopher too, as the media discovered when India were touring New Zealand in March 2009. India were on the verge of winning a Test series there after forty years. The last time India had won a series (which was also India's first ever Test series abroad) was in 1968 when the late Nawab of Pataudi was the captain.

Before the Napier Test, the Indian team was in Auckland, instead of being at Napier, the venue. When the media confronted Dhoni with this unusual situation, he turned philosophical and answered, "if you tell the mind it is Napier, the mind perceives it as Napier, that is the mind accepts what it is fed because it is an abstract entity." There you have it, Dhoni in a philosophical mood!

When asked specifically if it was all right to be in Auckland when the team should have been in Napier, planning for the match, he replied, "We are not thinking about the series; not even about this Test per se. We are just focussed on the first session on the morrow."

In a similar vein, he explained that the form of a batsman too is an abstract. He said people talk about a player being "in form", but no one has seen form, because it is a state of mind when one feels confident, one feels one can achieve what one has thought about.

Understandably, the media, including senior reporters, were flabbergasted.

In the course of that interaction he also added, "We don't plan for too long. We believe in focusing on the small steps, on the immediate goals. We know that will take care of the big picture."

The reports that appeared on 26 March in the country's leading newspapers were not very flattering. The reports described him as "Captain Philosopher", and one headline read, "Path, not goal, is now in Team India's vision," and yet another report said, "Dhoni turns philosopher ahead of the Napier Test." One senior reporter wrote that Dhoni showed human frailty at the end of the press conference when he uttered, "Touchwood! It remains the same," referring to the good atmosphere in the dressing room where everyone got on well with others.

Indeed, in an interview to a newspaper, talking about his goal as a captain, as a batsman and as a wicketkeeper, he said he doesn't have any goals. For him, "it's always about the next match."

That is how he sees cricket. He has said many times that he draws his strategy after getting on the field, after assessing the playing conditions and having a look at the wicket. More than theory he believes in practice.

Doesn't this cool captain with steely calmness, ever get nervous? He does. But as he says, "At the start of a big game you are a bit nervous, that nervous energy is very good, you focus and do well."

***

15
Discipline and Confidence

Discipline and confidence, on or off the cricket field, define Dhoni. A 'no problem child' to his parents, he remained a 'no problem player' to his teams and captains and a 'no problem student' to his teachers at school.

Since his childhood, there has been no recorded or reported instance of an act of indiscipline on his part.

This invaluable asset has taken him from the rough grounds of district level cricket to the lush green international stadia, from dimly lit cheap hotel rooms to luxurious rooms at five star hotels.

Even the internationally acknowledged cricket experts, who do not tire of calling him 'captain cool' and 'captain courageous', have never found fault with him in matters related to discipline, on or off the field. Dhoni enjoys an impeccable record in this.

However, if refusing an offer by Ranji selectors can be described as an act of indiscipline, then he was guilty of one such transgression when he turned down the selectors in 2004. They wanted that he should lead Jharkhand in Ranji trophy matches.

Instead of grabbing that opportunity, he told the selectors that he wanted to concentrate on his wicket keeping and batting. May be he did not want any thing to distract him from his goal, which was playing for India.

Recalls Pradeep Khanna, India under-25 player and then a Ranji selector, “In 2004 we, the Ranji selectors, offered him the captaincy of the state team, but he refused saying he wanted to concentrate on his game and improve it further.”

That shows how meticulously and with a clear focus he had been planning his cricket career. Like Arjuna who saw only the eye of the fish, MSD too apparently had his eyes fixed on a place in Team India.

However, the rare instance of leading a team during that phase of his cricket career came up in 2000. This time it was an act of discipline and he obeyed the seniors in the district cricket administration. For an inter-district match against Palamau at Daltonganj, he was asked to lead the Ranchi District Cricket team, that too for a solitary match, because some of the senior players were not available. That appointment became controversial. It was not acceptable to one player, Anant Prakash, a Ranji player who refused to play under a player, who was not only junior to him by some years but was yet to play a Ranji match. Dhoni remained unaffected by that protest and told Debal Sahay, then chairman of the selection committee, that he need not worry as he would handle the seniors who were still in the team. Despite the absence of several senior players Dhoni led the Ranchi team to victory.

His team mates remember him as a focused player. Be it a practice session, or a match, or even an inconsequential match, he never took anything lightly. Recalls Adil Hussain, "Even in an inconsequential match he would take his batting and wicket keeping seriously. I never felt that I had to reprimand him for anything. He was very punctual and disciplined and worked really hard at the nets. An ideal team man." Shades of his idol Sachin Tendulkar!

Dhoni's teammate in Ranji matches and in the South Eastern Railway team for four seasons, Shashi Bhusan Choubey, a leg spinner, recalls, "During Ranji camps at Jamshedpur when we got a couple of days off, we used to take permission and rush home to Ranchi. But Dhoni used to stay behind in Jamshedpur and arrange for practice. Even during the Ranji match against Karnataka at Mecon stadium, the home team players were put up at Hotel Yuvraj. Those who belonged to Ranchi took permission to go home and report for the match in the mornings. But Dhoni again chose to stay with the team and participated in the exercise and practice sessions with the team, though his home was just yards from the stadium. He was so serious and committed. That is why, while many attribute his success to luck, I call it the result of his 'karm-pradhan', luck comes later."

Choubey was captain of the Ranchi District Cricket team in 2003, when Dhoni scored 154 runs not out against Dhanbad in the inter-district final and helped Ranchi, with a heavily depleted batting line up, save the match and share the trophy.

Another personality trait that Hussain found commendable in him was that he kept a low profile, and never chattered unnecessarily. Choubey too echoes that view. "He used to be very disciplined and serious on the field, and I never saw him indulge in unnecessary banter."

What is truly remarkable about him is the level of self-confidence. Hussain says, "I found him to be a very confident person. Whatever be the state of the match, he remained calm and composed, have never seen him getting ruffled. And he won many a match for us with his aggressive batting."

He adds, "Look at the way he conducts himself at the post match presentation ceremonies, the way he appeared when he shared the stage with Shah Rukh Khan at a Sahara function, or other such occasions. He never gives the impression that he is feeling uncomfortable. Rather, he gives the impression that he belongs there. For a cricketer from a place like Ranchi, it is amazing how confidently he conducts himself in all situations."

His Ranji team mate Santosh Lal recalls, "I cannot forget the cool and calm manner in which he walked out to bat against Kerala in a Ranji match after we had lost one too many wickets. He scored an aggressive 97 runs to bail our team out."

And the latest example of his level of confidence in his own ability was seen at Wankhede stadium on the evening of 2 April 2011, when he walked in to bat ahead of the in-form Yuvraj Singh and went on to score a match winning undefeated 91 runs in 79 balls and hit a six off Nuwan Kulasekara to win the Cup, 2011.

Discipline can be used as a synonym for his name. Even as a player of the district team or the CCL team, he was an model of discipline. Not only that, he always tried to persuade his team mates to follow the team discipline and not indulge in things that would affect their performance the next day.

"In those four years that he was with us, I never had to remind him of anything that he was asked to do, either on or off the field. Even for net practice, he was very punctual and worked hard at the nets," says the CCL captain Adil Hussain.

When this writer went to meet MSD after his first tour with Team India to Bangaladesh in December 2004, his mother said, "He used to come home from school, eat something and go out to run and play, then return home in time and sit down to study. He never gave any trouble. He was always disciplined."

Those long runs explain his powerful legs, stamina and his speed between the wickets while taking runs. Commentators Sunil Gavaskar and Ravi Shastri never fail to talk about his speed between wickets. After he comes to the crease the running between wickets picks up automatically.

He completed class XII with 56 per cent. That meant he had to seek admission under sports quota for a bachelor's degree in commerce at Gossner College in 1999.

Because of his growing cricket commitments, he never could complete the course. But his desire for a bachelor's degree remained. In August 2008, he revived his pursuit of a bachelor's degree by enrolling for a degree course in office management at St Xavier's College. That would lead to a bachelor's degree in Commerce.

By this time his star appeal made him a much sought after student. St Xavier's College decided to relax norms for him. He was exempted from attending classes. They agreed to supply him the course material for each semester, and agreed to arrange for examinations at a convenient place. Gossner College reluctantly issued him the college leaving certificate.

The St Xavier College authorities realised his star power when he visited the college in March, for admission. The entire college came to a standstill as thousands of students assembled on the college grounds to greet him.

Hectic cricket commitments have however, prevented him from taking any semester examination so far. His registration will be valid till 2013.

His teachers at school remember him as a shy and disciplined pupil. His Maths teacher KD Singh, however, admits he would reprimand him occasionally for missing classes though he knew that he did so for playing cricket. Which teacher would have guessed at that stage that Dhoni was destined to become such a big cricketer?

His games teacher Keshab Ranjan Banerjee, a qualified football coach from the National Institute of Patiala, was looking for a wicketkeeper for the school team. As football coaching was in session, Banerjee had observed he was a natural and good goal keeper. Hence, he asked him to switch over from football to cricket. As he was a good goal keeper, the switch over was easy. All Banerjee had to do was convince him that instead of a big ball, he would have to catch a much smaller ball. Thus the school cricket team got a wicketkeeper and a young boy was put on a path that would take him to the pinnacle of success in international cricket.

***

16
Likes and Loves

On 30 July in 2009, MSD drove his newly bought Hummer, the beast among four wheeled SUVs, into his home city. On the long drive home from Delhi, via Lucknow, the Indian fast bowler Rudra Pratap Singh was with him. Owning and driving a Hummer suits the rough and tough image of MSD.

Dhoni and his Hummer appeared on the radar of the local police, at Barhi, on the Grand Trunk road. From that point right up to his home then in the Shyamali colony, the Ranchi police escorted him. It was a secret mission; still the local media was alerted. Positions were taken on the national highway and lens men waited for hours. For all their efforts all they could catch was a glimpse of Dhoni's Hummer passing by, driven by a man who looked somewhat like him.

In the last two years that Hummer has not been seen by his fans. Only once, it was reported that Dhoni and his friends had been to the Deori temple in the Hummer.

Around the same time, off spinner Harbhajan Singh too had bought a Hummer. Some electronic news channels showed Harbhajan posing with his new acquisition and they also reported that he was charged with driving around without the mandatory registration number by an over zealous official.

In Dhoni's case, his Hummer has remained under wraps.

But acquiring a Hummer, soon after acquiring a burly and handsome Harley Davidson, to add to his long list of power-packed motorcycles proves just one thing: he earns in crores and indulges his passion without any inhibition.

His stable comprises, besides the Hummer and Harley Davidson, motorcycles like Kawasaki ZX4, Ninja, a Royal Enfield, and a number of TVS motorcycles as he is the brand ambassador for TVS. He cannot ride the Harley Davidson through the congested traffic of his home city, so he goes for early morning rides on the VIP road, which is wider and almost empty in the early hours of the morning. But such rides have become rarer in recent times because of the hectic cricket schedule.

Though he loves power packed bikes, he is a careful driver. He is not a speed freak. Among four-wheelers, he has a Mitsubishi Pajero, a custom made Scorpio, a Scorpio and a Toyota Corolla that was gifted by the Jharkhand chief minister Madhu Koda in 2007. Fond of bikes, he once revealed in an interview that he "loves dirt biking" and a motorcycle company had promised him a customized dirt bike. This love for bikes saw him feature in "Personal Best" in the Asian edition of Time magazine in 2007. Dhoni also loves animals. Sam, a German Shepherd of mixed parentage, has been his darling pet ever since he played for India. At home he loves spending time with Sam. After becoming famous, he brought home Zara, a black Labrador. At Harmu Colony these two are taken for their walks under the watchful eyes of security guards.

He has consented to adopt a tiger in Mysore, reportedly under the persuasion of former Test fast bowler Srinath. Back home, the state forest department is keen that he adopts a tiger at the Birsa Munda Zoo in Chakla, about 15-km from the city. He has also given his consent to be the brand ambassador for tiger conservation in Uttarakhand, the state from where his parents hail.

Computer games have been his obsession since his teenage days. Doctors recall how he would be busy playing games on his cell phone, sitting on the steps of Apollo hospital while his brother in law Gautam pursued his business affairs. His favourite computer games, by his own account, are "shooting games, counter strike, Black Hawk Down, Men of Valour…" etc.

Listening to Hindi songs, particularly those sung by Lata Mangeskar and Kishore Kumar, is a favourite pastime. He doesn't enjoy English songs. He loves being in jeans and a T-shirt. He feels most comfortable in informal dress though he looks smart in suits.

As a boy he may have been a vegetarian but these days he loves his chicken tikka. For relaxation, when he is at home, he spends quite a lot of time with his pet dogs, Sam and Zara. Quite often he takes out his air gun to practice target shooting. At Shyamali colony he practices target shooting in the courtyard.

He has a passion for firearms. He has a license for a 7.65 mm non-prohibitory bore pistol and the license for a 9 mm prohibited bore pistol is in final stages. "Football was my first love and I still play football in the off season", he once told young boys and girls in an interview.

In football he was a goalkeeper who was not afraid of diving and sliding, whatever be the surface, to stop the ball. These days when he plays some fun football, he plays as a forward. He even scored a goal while playing in a Dhoni XI versus Sudesh Mahto XI, an exhibition football match at the Silli Sports Academy.

Banerjee says, "Mahi used to be a good badminton player. In the under-16 age group he had reached quarters finals at the open Mohan Ahuja badminton tournament held at Jamshedpur in the undivided days of Bihar. Even after becoming a Test player, he would come to the school, park his SUV hidden inside the campus, and play badminton in the indoor hall." Perhaps, given his commitment to cricket, he played those long sessions of badminton to keep himself fit.

His love for badminton was also telecast on news channels when he spent some time at Lucknow and played badminton with his team mate R P Singh. His teacher Banerjee says Dhoni is "a total sportsman", who even played basketball and participated in the inter-house basketball matches. It's just destiny that Dhoni took to cricket when his school team needed him, otherwise given his commitment he could have excelled in either football or badminton.

As Dhoni himself once told the youngsters, "It's just that I loved playing more than studying."

But he does read books. Though he is not an avid reader, these days he carries books on wars and battle strategies.

***

A winning smile: Early days

Playmates:
Sam and Zara

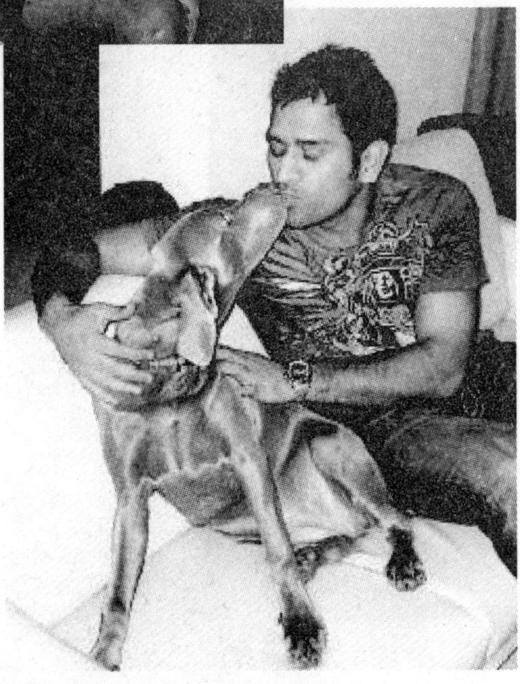

Favourite pastime:
His love for bikes competes with his love for soccer

Ardent admirers: Dhoni with chief minister of Jharkhand Arjun Munda (2010), (top), Pakistan's former President Pervez Musharraf (2006) (centre), and children at a school.

With wife, greeting fans from the balcony

uccess or failure, it's always the eori Temple near Ranchi he visits.

A hair stylist's delight

17
How Others See Him

Mahendra Singh Dhoni has become such an iconic figure, a symbol of hard work and success that even a state government and its officers are asked by a chief justice to emulate his "enthusiasm and zeal."

On 4 April 2011, two days after Dhoni had led India to the World Cup victory, chief justice of Jharkhand High Court Bhagwati Prasad was hearing PILs on encroachments and illegal occupation of public land.

In the course of the hearing he was reported to have commented, "Dhoni single-handedly turned the World Cup final match in favour of the country at a very difficult moment. Such enthusiasm and zeal should be present in the government and its officers; this will put the state on the national arena."

The Chief Justice added, "Jharkhand has witnessed three major developments. First, the panchayat elections held after 32 years. Second, the 34th national games, and now the son of the soil Dhoni has brought the World Cup. It re-iterated the cherished history of Jharkhand from Jaipal Singh to Mahendra Singh Dhoni."

That was a very apt summation of the sporting history of the state of Jharkhand where both Jaipal Singh and MS Dhoni were born.

The Oxford-educated legendary tribal leader Jaipal Singh was the captain of the Indian hockey team that won the gold medal at the 1928 Olympic Games. That was India's first gold medal in the Olympic Games.

Dhoni, of course, has led India to victory in the Cricket World Cup 2011 at Wankhede stadium for India's second World Cup title 28 years after India, led by Kapil Dev, in 1983 stunned the favourites West Indies to bring the Cup home. Dhoni's leadership qualities have drawn praise from every quarter.

Former Pakistan captain Zaheer Abbas wants Shahid Afridi to learn from him how to bat responsibly when leading Pakistan.

Abbas said, "Shahid Afridi needs to learn from Indian captain MS Dhoni, who was a pinch hitter earlier but ever since he became captain he does not throw his wicket away." These days we see him relying more on 1s and 2s, rotating the strike and consolidating, a strategy that has bailed out the Indian batting many times.

Three years earlier, another former Pakistan captain Asif Iqbal had said if he had a team he would definitely love to have him as its captain.

A year before, former England captain Nasser Hussain had commented that as a team reflects the style and attitude of its captain, the Indian team is starting to reflect Mahendra Singh Dhoni a little, in an extravagant and outgoing manner.

Hussain pointed out how the players, under Dhoni, celebrated everytime a wicket fell, and how a bowler got support on the field even when he got caned.

Former Australian captain Alan Border confesses he is a big fan of Dhoni and sees him as a man of "steely calmness." Add to this, Imran Khan's "he's got courage, he's got guts."

Border led Australia to the World Cup title in 1987. On his part it was a gutsy move to come on to bowl his left arm spinners against a well-settled England captain Mike Gatting, who was batting so well that England seemed on course for the World Cup title; till Gatting played that reverse sweep against Border and was caught out. England batting collapsed and they lost yet another World Cup final.

Imran Khan, himself an example of guts, came out to bat at number three, set an example and laid the foundation of a good score. His moves saw England lose yet another World Cup final, this time in Australia in 1992.

After winning the World Cup 2011, Sachin Tendulkar described him as "a fabulous captain" who is "calm and patient, but at the same time, he's very clever and shrewd… very, very alert." Tendulkar added that Dhoni's situational awareness is his biggest strength, and he knows the likes and dislikes of every individual team member. That indeed is wholesome praise coming from a great cricketer like Sachin Tendulkar.

Former India player and commentator Ravi Shastri, with whom Dhoni has had a couple of witty exchanges at the post match presentation ceremonies, describes him as "one who never loses his composure" and who does not allow his body language to give anything away.

One recalls how his facial expressions gave away Sourav Ganguly's feelings when as captain of Team India he found the match slipping out of his hands. Equally well documented is his spontaneous reaction at Lord's after the Natwest ODI final in 2002 when he took off shirt and waved it around after Yuvaraj Singh and Md Kaif took India to victory, in a match that had been all but lost.

But such betrayals of emotions are rare in Dhoni's case. One such concession to emotion was seen at Dharamshala in the Indian Premier League III in 2010. In a do or die match for Chennai Super Kings, Dhoni batted aggressively and after hitting the winning runs pumped his fists. Chennai went on to win IPL III defeating Mumbai Indians, led by his cricketing idol Sachin Tendulkar.

Except those rare occasions, he does convey a steely calmness. His friend and cine star John Abraham should have the final say on him. To him, Dhoni, or Mahi as he calls him, is the best cricketer in the world. "I don't think there is a better captain, batsman or wicketkeeper.... Mahi and I are friends for life. We'll be buddies even after his cricketing career and my run in films come to an end."

***

18

Controversies Timeline

2008: After losing the Asia Cup final against Sri Lanka in 2008, MSD spoke against too much cricket and opted out of the Test series in Sri Lanka, later joining the team for the ODI.

2009: Didn't attend the official ceremony at Rashtrapati Bhawan for receiving the Padmashree award. Harbhajan Singh, also an awardee that year, did not attend the function either.

2011: Citing too much cricket, pulled out of the T20 and ODIs in the West Indies, but joined the team for the Test series.

These three major controversies dot Dhoni's otherwise successful cricket career in the international arena. These rankled experts, former cricketers and his fans too.

His supporters hailed his outburst against too much cricket in 2008 and admired his guts at taking that decision, and in putting his place in the Test team at stake. For the Sri Lanka's tour, Dinesh Karthik and Parthiv Patel were chosen; both being wicket-keeper batsman, like Dhoni. His place in the Test squad would have been threatened if either of them had succeeded in cementing his place in the team. Fortunately for Dhoni, neither performed outstandingly in that Test series against Sri Lanka.

In his fans' perception, he emerged as a player who was unafraid of the Board of Control for Cricket in India (BCCI) bosses. No one, barring injury-scarred Sachin Tendulkar in recent years and a peeved Mansur Ali Khan, late Nawab of Pataudi, in 1970-71, had done it before. That was a gutsy decision and his supporters hailed it as such.

The late Nawab of Pataudi was dropped from captaincy for the historic West Indies tour in 1970-71, when India won its first ever series against the mighty West Indians, that too on their home turf. They won the second Test at Port of Spain, with four other Tests ending in a draw.

Pataudi was replaced by Ajit Wadekar by the casting vote exercised by the then chairman of the selection committee, the legendary Vijay Merchant, who, it was alleged settled some old score related to Pataudi's father, who too was captain of India when Merchant was an active Test player.

Ironically, in his autobiography Ajit Wadekar wrote that on the morning of the selection committee meeting he had phoned Pataudi. Wadekar himself was stunned in the afternoon when the news came that he was to replace Pataudi as captain of the Indian team.

It is a different story that under Wadekar India won its first ever Test series in the West Indies, then led by the greatest all rounder Sir Garfield Sobers. It was in this series that Sunil

Gavaskar made his debut in the second Test and scored more than 700 runs in four Tests, with four centuries 116 (3rd Test), 117 not out (4th Test) and 124 and 220 (5th Test) to announce his arrival.

However, Pataudi was to get back the captaincy in 1974 from Wadekar, whom the BCCI dumped after the disastrous tour of England, which is known as the 'summer of 42' as India were bowled out for 42 and went on to lose the series.

It was also ironical that Pataudi was asked to lead the team against the touring West Indies team, led by Clive Lloyd. Vivian Richards and Gordon Greenridge made their debut on this tour. India lost the first two Tests, at Bangalore and Delhi, won the third and 4th at Calcutta and Madras, but lost the final Test at Bombay.

Besides Pataudi, in recent years it has been Sachin Tendulkar who has been able to ask for rest from the hectic schedule so that he could tend to his various injuries, and on some occasions spend some time with his family.

Now Mahendra Singh Dhoni has joined that short list.

Dhoni's pulling out of the Test series in Sri Lanka in 2008 did not create a huge storm. But in 2011, his decision to pull out of the first part of the West Indies tour, when T20 and the ODIs were to be played did. It became the focal point when experts and former cricketers discussed the new trend among India players, who were willing to play all the matches in the Indian Premier League, even while nursing injuries, but asked for rest when it was time to do their duty for the country.

The 4th edition of IPL, 2011, ended on 28 May and the Indian team to the West Indies left on 31 night from Mumbai.

The World Cup 2011 had ended on 2 April, and IPL began on 8 April. It was indeed a very tight schedule. Too much cricket took its toll.

Dhoni, after leading the Chennai Super Kings to the second consecutive IPL title, said at the post match ceremony that for the first five days he would go to Ranchi. Though he had been in the country for the last four months he had not visited home. He also told the media that it was tough to play in the IPL soon after the World Cup.

Virendra Sehwag had already left for England to get his injured shoulder repaired surgically. The shoulder injury of Gauatm Gambhir surfaced during the IPL. He had been chosen to lead India in the T20 and the ODIs, but had to be replaced by a red faced BCCI. In his place Suresh Raina was asked to lead Team India. Sachin Tendulkar first pulled out of the T20 and the ODIs, and subsequently from the Test series too. Yuvraj Singh too, pulled out because of upper respiratory tract infection. The BCCI had already announced rest for the left arm fast bowler and backbone of the Indian attack, Zahir Khan. Dhoni also had pulled out of the first part of the West Indies tour.

Thus, Team India was to travel to the West Indies without Sehwag, Gambhir, Tendulkar, Yuvraj Singh, Zahir Khan and MS Dhoni. With these being the best players, cricket fans were disappointed. All these missing stalwarts had played all the IPL matches that they and their respective teams had to play. Sehwag went off to England for treatment of his shoulder only after he realised the Delhi Daredevils had no chance of getting into the last four of the IPL, 2011.

Naturally, former India players and captains like Kirti Azad, Bishen Singh Bedi, Sunil Gavaskar, Farooq Engineer and others were constrained to discuss the question–Club over country–on an electronic news channel.

In those discussions Dhoni's name cropped up frequently. Maybe, it would not have if he were the only one to pull out, like it had been in 2008. But this time, with as many as five top players pulling out, it was difficult to ignore such a development.

Outspoken Bishan Singh Bedi went on to tell *The Telegraph*, an English daily, that "Dhoni will take a break from international cricket but you bet he won't rest while turning out for the Chennai Super Kings, which is controlled by the president-elect of the BCCI, Srinivasan."

Bedi described the players as 'slaves' bought at an auction by the team owners, and, therefore, 'they can't have any rights'. Sunil Gavaskar said, "It's the player's prerogative whether he wants to rest during the IPL or a Test series." But he asked the selectors to act tough and drop those who opt out. Here Gavaskar had cricket history backing his sentiment.

Though Gavaskar is known as one who fought against the BCCI persistently for more remuneration to players, and has always defended players making more money for a secure post cricket life, he had chosen to play for the country, and not for a team in the Packer series of cricket in Australia, which would have fetched him more money than the BCCI was paying to its players then. In some ways the IPL reminds one of the Kerry Packer series of cricket that was organized by Kerry Packer, the owner of Channel 9, in Australia in the late 1970s. The only difference between the Packer series and the IPL is that while the former was a 'rebel series', the IPL is the favourite son of the BCCI, who is enriching his parent body.

Sunil Gavaskar and Bishan Singh Bedi belonged to that era when "country came first" even though the BCCI used to pay a pittance to the players. Bedi recalled getting Rs 750 for five days of Test cricket. Prior to that Rs 250 was paid for five days of Test cricket, and once Rs 50 was deducted from the match fee because the Test match had ended in four days.

In 1978-79, the Packer series reared its commercial head, lured top players like Ian Chappel, Greg Chappel, Vivian Richards, Clive Llyod, Asif Iqbal, and many others from Test playing countries. Those who played in the Packer series were banned by their respective national cricket boards. Australia recalled Bobby Simpson from retirement to lead Australia against India in 1979-80. In the West Indies, Clive Llyod as captain, was replaced by Alvin Kalicharan.

During the 1978-79 tour of Pakistan, a Kerry Packer agent approached the Indian stars, such as Sunil Gavaskar, too. He refused to become a part of the series.

Consequent to a fight over telecast rights, Kerry Packer floated the Packer World Series. Coloured clothes and cricket under lights were the highlights of that series. Later, a compromise was reached and remuneration to players was enhanced by the respective national cricket boards. But undeniably, the Packer series changed the face of international cricket. IPL too is doing this, or has already done it. Will this change be for the better, or for worse for cricket? Time alone will answer.

However, two days before the IPL IV final on 28 May, the former cricketers argued that players these days were more committed to their clubs because the franchisees paid them in crore. Hence, playing for their country had become secondary, otherwise, how could a player pull out from Team India citing fatigue from too much cricket and yet continue to play all 15 matches in IPL, soon after a gruelling schedule of the World Cup. Kirti Azad, a member of the team that won the World Cup in 1983, questioned: "What about commitment by God of cricket, playing for Mumbai Indians with a split arch and captain Dhoni, and Zaheer Khan, not going to West Indies and continue playing in IPL."

Bedi wondered, "If three or four players are tired, why seven or eight others are not tired?" He targeted the BCCI for letting things come to this stage.

They also argued like former chief selector Kiran More, 'when you represent your country you become a superstar, and then you get money and command respect.'

As an example, Sourav Tiwary was bought by the Royal Challengers for around seven crore because he had played in three ODIs for India, whereas a player like Manish Pandey was bought for much less. The label of being an India player does matter.

Union sports minister Ajay Maken too joined the issue when he said he would like players to play for the country first and then the clubs.

As IPL is a subsidiary of the BCCI and its secretary and president designate N Srinivasan is the owner of Chennai Superkings led by MS Dhoni, the former cricketers and captains demanded that BCCI should come clean on this aspect.

Some of them argued that sending a second team to the West Indies was putting India's reputation at stake; others argued that telecasters would not be happy with a second India team, sans stars like Sachin and Dhoni, as it would discourage sponsors, which would affect the series financially too.

This "club over cricket" issue involved cricketers from other countries too. Lasith Malinga announced his retirement from Test cricket because "he had a bad knee and wanted to prolong his cricket career by abstaining from the longer version of the game." Thus, he opted out of the Sri Lanka tour of England that was to begin before the IPL 2011 ended on 28 May 2011.

Chris Gayle, the former West Indian captain and an explosive opening batsman, too opted to play for the Royal Challengers, Bengaluru, in the IPL than in the series against Pakistan, in the same period. But his decision may also have had something to do with the West Indian cricket board.

On this contentious issue Peter Roebuck, in his column in *The Hindu,* wrote, "Increasingly prominent players are letting down their countries and the game at large. Fit for their IPL clubs, or rather franchises (and there's the rub) they withdraw from international commitments pleading exhaustion or injury."

Roebuck went on to comment, in the context of five top Indian players pulling out of the West Indies tour, 'sending a reduced team indicates that international cricket is in a perilous state. Personal desire has replaced public service.'

He also commented that the West Indies, remained one of the few strongholds of cricket and was in urgent need of uplift, but by sending a reduced team India had 'snubbed it'.

Another development that stirred the former cricketers was that the BCCI requested the Sri Lankan board to allow the Sri Lankan players, like Mahela Jayawardne, (who were playing in the IPL), to report late to the Sri Lankan board for the England tour.

Former cricketers cited this as an example of the BCCI's attitude and alleged that the Board was encouraging players to prefer IPL because this tournament was filling up the BCCI coffers. Suddenly, the question–Club over Country–acquired serious proportions, involving the Indian as well as some players from other countries. Certainly this question will continue to be discussed hereafter too.

The third major controversy that Dhoni stirred was when he did not attend the official ceremony at Rashtrapati Bhawan to receive the Padmashree from the President. Local newspapers reported that Dhoni was to fly to Delhi for the function. He did fly out of Ranchi, but his destination was not Rashtrapati Bhawan in Delhi. Why he did not attend, or could not attend? Dhoni alone would be able to answer these questions. He did not issue any clarification, even though allegations surfaced in the media that he had some endorsement engagement.

He ignored all insinuations and adverse reports that followed in the media. He did not issue any statement on this issue. Perhaps that was his way of handling controversies.

Consequently, the Padmashree was sent by post to the state government. It was on 22 September 2009, that Dhoni went to the office of the then chief secretary to receive the award.

***

19 Dhoni's Moments of Agony

As Mahendra Singh Dhoni is a normal human being, his career as a cricketer has had some dark and agonizing moments too.

Take his debut for India in the first one-day international against Bangladesh at Chittagong on 24 December 2004, where he was run out for a zero. His friends will tell you how he hates getting out, particularly run out. When he was playing a domestic match at Bokaro, while batting for Ranchi, he was run out because of a mistake in calling for a run by his partner. He smashed his bat into pieces and swore he would not play cricket any more. At Chittagong, however, he must have exerted internally to restrain himself from giving vent to his anger and frustration.

Or, take those three ODIs in his debut series. He could barely score 19 runs. For an ambitious and run-hungry young batsman, who was pursuing his dream, the days following that series must have been full of agony.

But he got back to scoring runs in his inimitable style in the second ODI against Pakistan at Vishakapatanam on 5 April 2005, with 148 runs. This was to become vital in cementing his place in Team India. As Dhoni said in an interview, that innings secured his place in Team India for another 12 to 14 matches, enough to motivate him to perform without fear – a pre-condition for success.

But agony was waiting for him at the World Cup 2007, in the West Indies. India were humbled and humiliated by Bangladesh and Sri Lanka, and were sent home early. In both these vital matches Dhoni could not score a single run.

An agonised Dhoni assembled his cricket friends and practised hard for hours to prepare for the Bangladesh tour. He played some match winning knocks and was adjudged man of the tournament. The newly introduced World Cup cricket tournament in the T20 format was to bring him glory, and agony too.

When he led India to the T20 World Cup title at Johannesburg in South Africa in September 2007, he was hailed as the new hero the cricket fans in the country were waiting for. He was leading a team of youngsters. No one expected anything from that team for two reasons.

Firstly, players like Sachin Tendulkar, Rahul Dravid and Sourav Ganguly had declined to play in the T20 World Cup. Secondly, till then India had played only one T20 match at the international level against South Africa. Though India managed to win that match by five wickets, courtesy some enterprising batting by Dinesh Karthik, who top scored with 31 not out, the team was not very familiar with this format.

Later, it was heard that even the BCCI bosses had not believed that the young team led by a rookie captain Dhoni, would do so well. The team's hotel bookings and travel plans had to be revised as India progressed further and further in the tournament.

That is why, those close to Dhoni suspected he was being made the sacrificial goat when asked to lead India. They were worried that if India failed, Dhoni's tenure in Team India would be cut short. But he took to captaincy and its responsibilities like he had been a veteran captain all his life.

When the same Dhoni could not take his team to victory in the second ICC T20 World Cup 2009, critics started looking for chinks in his strategy. His on-field decisions were scrutinized and questioned.

The defending T20 World champions could win against Bangladesh and Ireland only. South Africa beat us by 12 runs, the West Indies beat us by seven wickets, and England defeated us by three runs.

India lost to South Africa on 16 June 2009 by 12 runs in a do or die match. This was followed by the trade mark reaction of emotional fans. In Dhoni's hometown, his effigies were burnt. Experts questioned why Ravindra Jadeja was sent to bat ahead of Yuvraj Singh, and why he was selected ahead of Pragyan Ojha, another left arm spinner? Why the captain decided to chase rather than set a target against a strong team like South Africa?

When India's miserable performance at the Twnety-20 World Cup continued in its 2010 edition too, many were getting ready to write him off as a good captain. Experts said the captain with the Midas touch was losing his golden touch.

Of the five matches that India played in the T20 World Cup 2010, it won only two; the first against Afghanistan and the second against South Africa. Then followed three straight defeats: against Australia by 49 runs, against the West Indies by 14 runs, and finally, against Sri Lanka by five wickets.

Interestingly, in all these three matches Dhoni won the toss; against Australia he chose to field, but lost. In the match against the West Indies he won the toss and decided to field first, but again lost. Against Sri Lanka too he won the toss and elected to bat first but lost the match. It was a bad phase, as whatever decision he took, he went wrong.

That is how it happens in cricket, which has very often been described as an unpredictable game. In the inaugural edition of ICC T20 World Cup 2007, it was the same Dhoni, who leading a cricket team for the first time, could do no wrong.

Against Pakistan, in the league stage, we won in the "bowl out", with Dhoni's selection of bowlers being spot on. In the final match, his decision to give the last over to medium pacer Joginder Sharma was a shocking but bold, gutsy and intuitive decision. Starting with a wide, and then being hit for a six by Misbah-ul-Haq, loss seemed imminent, but for the fancy shot by Misbah that ended in a catch to Sreenath. India won the first T20 World Cup. A new leader in cricket India was born.

But in the subsequent ICC T20 World Cups, in 2009 and 2010, nothing went right for Dhoni and his boys. Another moment of agony for Dhoni must have been the Asia Cup 2008, in Pakistan, organised under the aegis of Asia Cricket Council (ACC).

India surrendered tamely to Sri Lanka, losing the final by 100 runs. The strong Indian batting line up, excluding Dhoni who scored 49 runs, could not fathom the 'carom ball' and other variations unleashed by the Sri Lankan spinner Ajantha Mendis. In an intelligent move, the Sri Lankans did not field Mendis against India in the inconsequential match in which both these teams had qualified for the finals.

Sri Lanka had piled up a huge score of 273 in 49.5 overs, courtesy a belligerent century by Sanath Jaisurya. In reply, India were bowled out for 173 in 39.3 overs as Ajantha Mendis appeared unplayable and took five wickets for 13 runs.

However, Dhoni and India made amends in the tenth edition of the Asia Cup, held in Sri Lanka in 2010. In the finals, India defeated the host team Sri Lanka comfortably by 81 runs. This time Sri Lanka could not play through the 50 overs as they were bowled out for 187 in the 45th over, in reply to India's 268 for five wickets in 50 overs.

This victory meant India had won the Asia Cup after a gap of 15 years; it was last won in 1995. With this win India became the Asia Cup holder for the fifth time, a record eclipsing Sri Lanka's four wins. It was yet another feather in Dhoni's cap as captain. He truly knows how to overcome the agony of failure and bounce back.

***

20
Dhoni's Ranchi

In 2007, when the Indian team was playing in England, and Dhoni was playing a match saving innings, one of the English commentators said, "Dhoni comes from Ranchi, a small hamlet."

That was an understatement. Many would argue that Ranchi and Jharkhand have become better and widely known after Dhoni started creating ripples in international cricket.

But Ranchi has been a major commercial and industrial centre, an educational hub, and a city that is fast acquiring the traits of a metropolitan city. Now it is developing as a major sports centre too.

It is the only city in Jharkhand with air links to Delhi, Mumbai and Kolkata, and other cities, through major airlines. This facility will be an important factor when the city is ready to host an international cricket match.

Some historians hold the view that the name Ranchi derives

from the Mundari word "aranchi", which means a short stick used for driving cattle. Mundari is the language of Munda, one of the major tribal communities in Jharkhand.

For the East India Company and the British it was an important centre militarily and administratively. In 1834, this city was known as "Kishanpur", named after Wilkinson, who was the first agent to the Governor General of the Lower Provinces. Locals used to call Wilkonson "Alkissun Saheb". Gradually, it came to be known as Ranchi.

In 1845, four German Christian missionaries came. Red bricked Cathedrals and churches and educational institutions followed. The second World War brought commerce to this city because it was an important military centre, with a military cantonment at Doranda. It is in Doranda that Mecon's Shyamali Colony is located, where Dhoni was born in 1981 and where he lived for about 28 years before moving to his home, "Shaurya", at Harmu Housing colony.

However, today it is the capital of the decade-old Jharkhand. Before this state was carved out of Bihar in November 2000, Ranchi used to be the second capital of Bihar. Till the 70s, it was also known as the summer capital. It overlooks the Chotanagpur plateau from a height of 2200 feet above sea level, and it has been a popular health resort. The rich and the affluent from major cities like Kolkata used to come here during the summer season, both for escaping the heat and humidity as well as for recovering from ailments like tuberculosis.

Besides Dhoni, Ranchi figures on the national as well as the international map for major industrial establishments. First and foremost among them is the Heavy Engineering Corporation (HEC), a dream project of Pandit Jawahar Lal Nehru, the first prime minister of the country. HEC was set up in collaboration with the USSR and Czechoslovakia as "the mother of heavy industries". Hindustan Steel Limited (HSL), predecessor of the Steel Authority of India Limited (SAIL) too is here. So was National Coal Development Corporation (NCDC), which subsequently gave way to Coal India Limited, formed after nationalization of the coal industry. Today, two important CIL subsidiaries, Central Coalfields Limited (CCL) (which shaped Dhoni's cricketing career to a great extent) and Central Mine Planning and Design Institute (CMPDI) are based here. In the private sector, Usha Martin industries started off here.

Though an industrial and commercial centre, Ranchi is surrounded by water falls and picnic spots. Within a radius of 45 kilometre, you can enjoy water falling from a height of 320 feet at Hundru Falls, from 144 feet at Dasam Falls, from 280 feet at Sita Falls, and 140 feet at Gautam Dhara or Jonha Falls. You can also drive 70 kilometre from the city to Hirni Falls, where water falls from a height of 120 feet.

Apart from the water falls surrounding the city, a drive out of the city in any direction takes you to a picturesque picnic spot - nature's gift that the state's tourism department is yet to exploit fully. Dhoni and his friends often used to drive down on their motorcycles to the Deer Park for an impromptu picnic or to get away from the school.

If this city lacked anything, from a cricketing point of view, it was infrastructure for cricket. As mentioned elsewhere in this book, cricket was played seriously but on hard and ill-maintained grounds, mostly on matting wickets. Even today there are only four turf wickets to cater to over 150 matches a season and most of the cricket is still played on matting wickets.

This could have been because the state cricket association, with headquarters in Jamshedpur, focused mainly on facilities for that city.

It was in 1984 that the city got its first turf wicket, at the Mecon Stadium, where the city hosted its first Ranji match, between Orissa and Bihar, 24-26 November, 1984. Dhoni was just three years old then. His father, Pan Singh, had helped in preparing this wicket.

Thereafter, Dhoni's home town has hosted 17 Ranji matches, one Wills Trophy match, one Deodhar trophy, and two Ranji Trophy super league matches.

Today, Jharkhand State Cricket Association's international stadium, is fast nearing completion. It has everything that would be required to host an international match.

The city has already hosted the 34th national games at the Jaipal Singh Mega Sports complex. This complex is unique in the sense that it comprises as many as nine stadia, with each capable of hosting an international meet. From athletics, to aquatics, from badminton to shooting, basketball, volleyball, wrestling, kho-kho, lawn tennis, table tennis… this complex has been hailed by the national sports federations. In days to come, we can expect more international and national sports meets being held here as this city now has all the required facilities, including hotels.

Dhoni's birth place is, thus, not a small hamlet by any stretch of the imagination. He once described it as a fast growing city, a metropolis in the making because of the diversity of its population and the growing commercial activities. These, together the beauty of nature surrounding it, make it a special city.

***

21 Dhoni's Endearing Qualities

'Who is he? Do you recognize him?' Dhoni was asked while being introduced to the Eastern Coalfields Limited players, who were playing the final match of the first Coal India T20 cricket tournament at Mecon stadium in February 2010.

Dhoni responded, "*Manjhi Da, kaise hain*?" (Manjhi Da, how are you?). Recalling this simple incident, Adil Hussain says, "It was amazing. Dhoni was seeing this player after almost a decade." He had played for CCL for four years, 1998 to 2002. For Dhoni to recall a player after so many years, that too after attaining such success in international and Indian cricket, was heartwarming. Manjhi was simply floored. Indeed, he will remain a fan of Dhoni forever.

Those close to him are right when they insist that he has got a very good memory and remembers even those whom he met during his stuggling days.

On one of his homecomings he drove down to the Archery ground to see his friend Santosh Lal play in a league match conducted by Ranchi District Cricket Association. Dhoni had played a number of matches on this ground before he started representing Team India. On that visit he walked up to the 'aloo-chana' vendor Mahendra, and addressed him, "kaise ho, Mahendra bhaiya, ek aloo-chana lagao" (How are you? Prepare one aloo-chana (potato-gram) with spices)-just as he used to do when he was just a budding player. This is the normal snack almost all players who play at the Archery ground eat in the course of a match because, apart from the team lunch, that is the only edible item available in the vicinity of that ground at Morabadi. Mahendra has served 'aloo-chana' chat to literally generations of players.

UK Jena, the curator of Mecon stadium, is another life-long fan of Dhoni. Whenever he visits the stadium, he makes it a point to meet him and other ground staff. Dhoni may not have played for Mecon, but he played many matches on this ground.

It was on this ground that he practiced for hours with his Ranji friends after the disappointing World Cup, 2007. He was determined to do well on the Bangaldesh tour, and he did well there. He bailed India out from embarrassment in the ODI at Mirpur, scoring 91 runs off 106 balls to take the team past Bangladesh's 250 runs. He went on to be adjudged the man of the tournament. What his peers and his seniors from the good old days of cricket in Ranchi and hereabouts like about him is that "he is still so grounded", does not have airs and does not behave like an international cricket star.

That is precisely what the players of South Eastern Railway team felt on the inaugural day of the T20 cricket tournament organized in February 2011 by Mahendra Singh Dhoni Charitable Trust, in tandem with Rhiti Sports management, who are now looking after his endorsements. Dhoni flew in for a day just before the ICC Cricket World Cup, 2011. He inaugurated the tournament and spent about half an hour in the team's dressing room, exchanging pleasantries and giving tips. The senior Railway players were happy that despite being so much in demand, he chose to be with them; the new players were excited to meet their hero.

His team mates at 'South Eastern Railways' Kharagpur base recalled, (while talking to an English daily), how Dhoni, who was unwell still came down to meet them in the hotel lobby of a five star hotel at Calcutta when they sent a message. They recalled, they found him behaving as he used to, when he stayed and played with them for the two years that he was posted at Kharagpur, as a ticket collector.

Back at Kharagpur, visualize a young Dhoni, about twenty years old, standing at the exit of Kharagpur railway station to catch those travelling without a valid ticket. Imagine how he must have felt in the earlier days of his duty as a ticket collector when he went to put the surrendered tickets into the box, and found many currency notes too. Obviously, during rush hours when it is not possible to check each and every ticket and the collector's hands get full in a few minutes, many passengers, while rushing through the exit, pushed some crumpled currency notes into his palm instead of a ticket. A bewildered Dhoni did not know what to do with those currency notes. But he found a way out of that tricky situation. He put all those notes, along with the tickets surrendered at the end of a journey into the box meant for used tickets!

While narrating this simple incident, the narrator, a former cricketer, emphasized the point that even in the face of such temptation Dhoni chose to play clean and fair. He could have pocketed those notes, but he did not. Either way no one would have known!

This attitude explains why under his captaincy the Chennai Super Kings have been able to win, along with the IPL IV title, the Fair Play award too.

Even those who are connected with his admission to St Xavier's College, Ranchi, for a degree course in Commerce, say they never got the impression that he wanted to acquire a graduation degree through a short cut. 'He gave the impression that he wanted to study for his degree, and not use his superstar status to just get a degree.'

One of Jharkhand's senior cricket coaches, Jai Kumar Sinha, was pleasantly surprised in 2008 when Dhoni visited him, and presented him with a bat. "For him to remember me and call on me, I'll never forget it. He has acquired such a stature that he need not have come to meet me. But he did. That shows his greatness," gushes Sinha. The bat presented to him has become his most prized possession.

Similarly, when Chanchal Bhattacharya, one of his earliest mentors, was injured in an accident, Dhoni promptly called on him. When Chanchal's father expired, Dhoni was away on cricketing duty, but his father attended the final rituals.

With his simplicity and gentle behaviour, Dhoni has won the hearts of almost every one he has interacted with during the course of his social meetings. After the birthday party of the son of a senior superintendent of police of his home town, everyone went back home very happy because Dhoni interacted with them and posed for photographs. "He is such a nice person," says the wife of a senior IAS officer. Her photograph with him is a prized possession, she said. A doctor's wife too recounted, at another social gathering, how well-behaved Dhoni was and how nice she felt being photographed with him.

The SSP had become so fond of him that when in July 2009 Dhoni was driving his Hummer, from Delhi to Ranchi, he personally received him before he entered the city.

The ministers of his home state too are happy. He responds to their invitations when they invite him for some felicitation function. One of them was candid enough to admit, "Coverage in the national media is assured on the electronic news channels if Dhoni is in the same frame." One of them, Bandhu Tirkey, Human Resource Development Minister, asked him to issue an appeal to children to come to school under the state government's "*Aao School Chale*" campaign. Dhoni readily agreed.

A *dhaba* owner on Ranchi-Jamshedpur route, on National Highway 33, recalls how as a young player Dhoni used to stop at his *dhaba* either on way to Jamshedpur for playing a match, or on his return journey. He accepted only tea free of cost, but made it a point to pay for his meal, Mukherjee, the dhaba owner recalls. In his early cricketing days he visited that *dhaba* a number of times, as did most of the players travelling to and from Jamshedpur for cricket matches, camps and selection trials.

Though these days Dhoni may not have the time to visit such *dhabas* and the smaller cricket grounds, yet when he comes across some one with whom he once interacted as an upcoming player, he recognizes and acknowledges them.

***

22 Dhoni's Brand Value

Less than a decade ago, as one of the eight stipend players of the CCL team, Mahinder Singh Dhoni was entitled to get Rs 40 a day as allowance while playing a match. This was in addition to the monthly stipend of Rs 2200.

While playing in matches at Sayal (a coal field area of CCL) he hit a lot of sixes so that he could collect more pocket money as each six was worth Rs 50.

These days one run scored by him in the IPL is estimated to be worth around rupees one and a half lakh!

There was a time too, when he booked a motorcycle, but as he did not have enough money for that high speed power bike, he said he would take the delivery after returning from the Pakistan tour, towards the last quarter of the 2005-06 season. He was such a success on that tour that when he returned from Pakistan, that motorcycle was given to him as a gift by the company.

After making his explosive batting talk in the second ODI

against Pakistan on 5 April 2005, he signed up with Calcutta based Gameplan Sports. Endorsements started coming his way.

But since the T20 World Cup victory in September 2007, his brand value has taken a quantum jump, and it has been since steadily rising....

A number of real estate developers have gifted him a flat in their residential complexes in Ranchi, Delhi and elsewhere.

Now business houses do not hesitate in signing him for a three-year contract and are willing to pay him huge amounts of money as high as Rs 26 crore for promoting their brand. He has joined the league of celebrities like Sachin Tendulkar and Shah Rukh Khan in endorsing products on television.

In July 2010, he signed a three-year deal with Rhiti Sports Management, headed by his friend Arun Pandey, and Mindscapes for Rs 210 crore.

He has more than two dozen brands in his kitty. Many more are likely to come since his brand value escalated after the World Cup 2011 victory.

Ad gurus such as Prahlad Kakkar and Alyque Padamsee describe him as a phenomenon, a youth icon, a national icon and one whose appeal covers a wide range, from five or seven-year-old children to their grandfathers.

They also caution that as Dhoni has achieved such stature, he should become selective in choosing products for endorsement.

His on-field performances, cool and calm demeanour as a captain, and his good looks, all combine to make him one of the hottest and most sought after brand ambassadors.

The fact that he has come from a humble background and risen to the top lends an aura to his personality that inspires millions of youngsters from a similar background, who have a living example of what any one of them can achieve with commitment, hard work and discipline.

When he sported a Samson-like long mane, several young boys imitated that style. It was usual to see groups of young boys with long hair moving around cities on motorcycles, and hanging around shopping complexes.

Once when he went to a hair dresser, thousands of boys and girls collected in that shopping mall. Dhoni had to remain locked in that salon for more than an hour till the police arrived to escort him out.

Since that day the hair dresser has been announcing concessions to customers, on the day Dhoni is slated to play in a final match or any important occasion like his birthday.

In September 2007, Sapna Bhawnani, a Bangalore-based hair stylist, convinced him to have his hair cut short. He continued to look good. Unlike Samson, who lost his strength when his hair was cut, Dhoni continued to court success. Youngsters back home followed suit.

Now that he is sporting the 'buzz' look, local salons have taken out their hair trimmers from the cupboards. You are now likely to see young boys and young cricketers with the 'buzz' cut.

He has become such a brand that even priests and astrologers try to piggy back on his stature. An amusing story was circulated when Dhoni shaved off his hair on 2 April night, after winning the ICC Cricket World Cup. Local newspapers carried reports that Dhoni was advised by such and such priest to get his hair cut done between 2 am and 3 am on 2 April night.

The very next morning, Dhoni told an English daily that there was no *mannat* or any such thing behind his decision to shave off his hair. He explained that with hot and humid weather in the offing and the IPL IV in tow, he just went and shaved off his hair. His wife Sakshi too admitted she was taken by a surprise when he came out of the bathroom whith his hair shaved off. No priestly advice there, obviously.

Even elitist clubs ride on his brand value and welcome him with open arms. In December 2007, Ranchi Club, his home town's oldest club established by the British, made him an honorary member and felicitated him. Members were very happy to have him as a guest at the New Year's party, where he joined them on the dance floor.

His brand value has now reached a stage when even educational institutions go out of their way to honour him.

At least two universities have shown interest in honouring him with an honorary doctorate degree. Soon after the World Cup 2011, Vinoba Bhave University at Hazaribagh in Jharkhand announced an honorary doctorate degree for him. Why not? 'Honorary doctorate degree is in recognition of some extraordinary achievement in any field', a sitting vice chancellor Dr Feroze Ahmed said. In April 2008, St Xavier's College was only too eager to enroll him as a student when Dhoni showed his desire for admission in that prestigious institution. Keeping his status in mind, they relaxed some rules and allowed him exemption from attending classes regularly.

Right from corporate houses to real estate developers to priests to educational institutions, all want to be linked, with Dhoni, whom cricket experts call "the man with the Midas touch," and whom the legendary Vivian Richards considers 'Mr Cricket'.

***

23
When Dhoni Is Home

Some one once said that the room at the top is lonely. In Dhoni's case it can be suitably modified to: "life in the room at the top is tiresome." Ever demanding fans and an ever intrusive media must be making it tiresome for him.

That conceivably is what Dhoni has to put up with whenever he comes home for a few days to rest after fulfilling his busy cricketing and endorsement commitments.

Consider his latest visit to his home town after attending the BCCI felicitation of the World Cup 2011, on 31 May at Mumbai. The very next afternoon, he landed at Ranchi airport with his wife Sakshi.

Fans and media chased him from the airport to his home. Every day of his stay here, fans gathered in front of his home. Some waited for a glimpse of their hero, some for his autograph. Some local newspapers too, deputed their photographers and reporters to keep a day long vigil at his home so that if he came out they could follow him. Such vigil led to some interesting stories related to his fans.

Among the crowd of fans was eight-year old Vansh from Kanpur, who was in Ranchi for a few days to meet his relatives. When he came to know Dhoni was in his home town, for two consecutive days he spent hours waiting outside 'Shaurya'. He could not meet him or see him. He went back to Kanpur disappointed. Sangita from Bokaro asked the security guard to take her autograph book inside and get it signed; a blank autograph book came back to her.

Passers by expose themselves to accidents as they look at his house, in the hope that they may get a glimpse of the cricket hero. On 3 June, two motorcycles rammed each other as one of riders was engrossed looking towards Dhoni's home.

Except for a brief appearance in his balcony after reaching home from the airport on 1 June, he remained confined the following two days.

Instead of going out, he calls over his close friends and relaxes with them. He also prefers to play computer games and spend time with his dogs, Sam and Zara, whenever home.

Once, his private time with his family was disturbed by a police officer, who shooed away the fans, threatening action against them. When the crowd at the entrance thinned out, he drove inside with his family so that they could meet Mr and Mrs Dhoni.

Another evening, the then state sports minister Sudesh Mahto dropped by and the two together made a brief appearance in the balcony for the benefit of the fans and the waiting photographers.

On 3 June, when he came out of 'Shaurya' late in the evening, driving his favourite Mitsubishi Pajero, fans and photographers surrounded him. Though he drove on, some photographers and reporters followed him to his farm house, which is under construction over a three acre plot at Simalia, some 15 to 17 kilometers away from the city.

Incidentally, Dhoni has planned a fast paced cricket pitch at his farm house. He is also to import a bowling machine from Australia so that when he is in his home town he can get some serious practice.

Though the photographers and reporters were not allowed to enter the farm house, their vigil continued. Next day it was reported in the local newspapers that Dhoni spent a quarter of an hour at the farm house with his friends. They had some snacks. Later, they had food at a '*dhaba*' and returned home around 11pm.

Despite keeping such a close watch on his movements, inaccurate reports frequently appear in the local media. For instance, it was reported that he would visit the Deori temple on 3 June. A horde of press reporters and photographers drove down about 50-km to the temple to wait for Mr and Mrs Dhoni but there was no trace of the Dhonis.

While his fans and the media chase him untiringly, the VIPs of his home town make their own demands on his time. Felicitations are organized at the drop of a hat, with flimsiest of excuses, and with eyes on wide media coverage across the country. Dhoni, and now his wife, and their family are obliged to attend such felicitations and mix with ministers, politicians and senior bureaucrats with their smiles in place.

It is on such occasions that the local media get a chance to ask him some questions. In such situations, Dhoni does interact with the media. But he smartly dodges tricky and controversial questions.

The sports department's original announcement, made on the completion of the 34th National Games on 26 February, was that all the medal winners from Jharkhand will be felicitated at a function which will be graced by Dhoni. In the meanwhile, Dhoni led India to the World Cup title and earned yet another felicitation himself.

But when Dhoni was available, 1-4 June, chief minister Arjun Munda was away in the USA for the treatment of his ailing son. Keeping in mind the fact that Dhoni would now be available only in July, or even later, the sports department arranged for a hurriedly organized function at the residence of Sudesh Mahto. At this hurriedly organized felicitation, the medal winners of the 34th national games were omitted for practical reasons.

Thus, while Dhoni was being felicitated at Mahto's residence on 4 June evening, India, led by Suresh Raina, were playing the T20 match against the West Indies. While S Badrinath and Rohit Sharma were taking India to a match winning score after a mini collapse, Dhoni was telling the media here that he loved Jharkhand, would like to set up a sports academy on the plot that the government was to gift him, and that academy would include other sports too. He was happy to have been made brand ambassador for environment protection, was happy India had a good bench strength and was number one.

That satisfied the media. The VIPs too went back happy, having spoken to him and being photographed with him.

On Sunday, 5 June, Dhoni paid his customary visit to the Deori temple in his Hummer, which hit the road after months of lying idle. As it was the World Environment Day, Dhoni planted some saplings too in the temple premises.

And the same afternoon, accompanied by Sakshi, he took the flight out of Ranchi.

***

24
Dhoni on Top

Following the victory in the final of the ICC World Cup 2011, the Institute of Finance and International Management, Bangalore, has included Dhoni in its curriculum. Students will be required to study the leadership qualities of Dhoni for their project report. He is perhaps the first Indian cricketer to feature in the curriculum of a business school.

Reacting to this development, Dhoni quipped during a felicitation function on 4 June in his hometown, "management institute students are going to study my mind."

Between 23 December 2004 and 2 April 2011, Dhoni has achieved so much within seven years, especially as a captain. Winning the inaugural ICC T20 World Cup 2007, may have been attributed to the proverbial beginner's luck but he followed that up with several astounding victories to silence his critics and win praise from virtually all the cricketing greats.

- 2 April 2011: The ICC Cricket World Cup title, along with the man of the final match for his unbeaten 91 runs off 79 balls.
- 28 May 2011: Chennai Super Kings wins the IPL for second successive year
- 2010: Asia Cup in Sri Lanka defeating Sri Lanka by 81 runs
- December 2009: India becomes number one Test team for the first time
- 2009: Padmashree
- 2008: The CB triangular series in Australia, defeating Australia 2-0 in the final series
- 2008: Rajiv Gandhi Khel Ratna Award
- 24 September 2007: ICC T20 World Cup title

What are the management students likely to find when they study his leadership qualities and prepare their project reports?

They are likely to find that he instills a sense of calm among players by remaining calm and cool himself in the worst situations during a match. Such calmness spreads among players, leading to a better performance, because a tense mind leads to a tense body and tense muscles, and a player's performance drops, as any sports psychologist would say.

They are also likely to find that he does not put his players under pressure. He only wants "commitment" and "if the commitment is there, it does not matter if a player had scored runs on a particular day or not." Dhoni asks his players to go out and give their best, show their commitment, and even if the result is not good, he, as captain, stands by them.

This approach takes away the fear of failure from a player's mind, and in all probability he is likely to perform better as he knows that one instance of failure would not throw him out of the team.

They are likely to find that he appears to be fair in finalizing the playing XI. Each player is included or omitted according to a well reasoned cricketing strategy keeping the best interest of the team in mind. That is why, he could suggest that he wanted "young legs" when the one-day team was being selected for the CB triangular series in Australia in 2008.

That stunning demand meant that senior players like Sourav Ganguly and Rahul Dravid were replaced by a couple of "young legs". India won the CB series, defeated Australia 2-0 in the finals and became the first Indian team to achieve that feat Down Under.

Later, after the World Cup 2011 victory, both Ganguly and Dravid heaped lavish praise on him for his leadership qualities.

They are likely to find that, as a leader, Dhoni does not run away from taking responsibilities on his own shoulders in a moment of crisis as he did in the final match of the World Cup. He walked out to bat ahead of an in-form Yuvraj Singh against Sri Lanka on 2 April night at Wankhede stadium.

He had not been getting high scores thus far in the World Cup. But as the situation demanded a decisive and inspirational move, Dhoni rose to the occasion. He had confidence in his own ability and more important, "fear of failure" did not exist in his vocabulary.

He must have known that if he had failed in his move, and

returned without scoring too many runs, sharpened knives would be waiting for him. But he did take the risk and it paid off.

Even as a school cricketer he had that quality. His games teacher at JVM Shyamali, KR Banerjee, recalls, "Dhoni used to bat at number seven or eight in the school team. But in that final against Central School, Hinoo, he insisted he would like to open the innings. I put a condition that if he wanted to open then he had better ensure that he did not get out and that he played through the innings." Dhoni did just that; he opened and remained unbeaten on 213 runs.

They, the management students, are also likely to find that if Dhoni takes a decision, he stands by it. If such a decision backfires, he readily admits it was a mistake, but does not blame anyone else for it. The most recent instance relates to the decision of playing a pace bowler instead of a spinner in the World Cup semi-final against Pakistan. At the post match presentation, he readily admitted he had misread the pitch at Mohali.

They are likely to find that he is frank and expresses his views in a polite manner, accompanied by a smile; whether the fielding was good or bad, whether bowlers performed well or not, or whether the batsmen let the team down or not. Though he expresses his views frankly, he does not publicly single out players who disappointed in a match.

His leadership qualities are visible in the way he has handled the players, some of whom, like Yuvraj Singh and Virendra Sehwag, senior to him and at one time strong claimants to the captaincy. But Dhoni must have handled their egos well to earn their commitment to the team's performance. He marshalled his resources so well and kept every player in such good humour that a temperamental Yuvraj Singh played like a man possessed, especially when hitting those five consecutive sixes in an over from the English fast bowler Stuart Broad.

Thus, it would not be wrong to assert that the Bangalore based management institute authorities have chosen the right man for a study of leadership qualities.

***

25
Superstition and Dhoni

"Seven" is a very important number in Dhoni's life and career as a cricketer. You will find this number on the back of his shirt in ODIs as well as the Indian Premier League.

The registration plate of his favourite SUV Mitsubishi Pajero is "Seven".

And his roll number, or call it registration number, at St Xavier's College, Ranchi, was 1105. Add all the numbers, it comes to "Seven". The college authorities were stumped when Ajay Nath Shahdeo, a close friend of Dhoni and deputy mayor of Ranchi Municipal Corporation, requested them for a roll number whose value should be "Seven", as this was his lucky number. The college teacher, who was in charge of the admission, had to do some calculation and adjustment to arrive at 1105. Reduced to a single digit, 1105 becomes "Seven".

And why not? It was on 7 August 2007, that the Board of Control for Cricket in India (BCCI) made him captain of the

Twenty-20 team for the inaugural ICC World T20 tournament in South Africa.

"Seven" is an important number in Dhoni's life because he was born on the 7th day of the 7th month of the year 1981: 07-07-1981.

He got engaged on 3 July and married on 4 July, in the 7th month, ie, July of 2010.

Superstition and cricket enjoy a very intimate relationship.

Which pad to put on first, or where to sit while watching a match on TV in one's drawing room, why players in the pavilion remain rooted to their seats and positions during tense moments in a match?

Former captain and swashbuckling opener Krishnamachari Srikkant explains this phenomenon, thus: '...despite the special skills in a cricketer, he often needs that something "extra" to sustain his self-belief.'

However, the best example of players remaining rooted to their seats and positions was recalled by Krish Srikkant. During the last league match against Zimbabwe at Tunbridge Wells in Kent during the Cricket World Cup in 1983, India were in a precarious position in that must win match, for a place in the semi-finals. The Zimbabwe seamers had reduced India to 17 runs for the loss of five wickets. The present Team India coach Duncan Fletcher was the main wrecker of the Indian innings.

The Indian captain Kapil Dev started batting confidently and with wicketkeeper Kirmani and all rounder Roger Binny, rescued India with unbeaten 175 runs scored off 136 balls and took the team's score to 266 for eight wickets.

During Kapil's heroic and historic innings, the highest individual score in a one-day international match, the Indian team's manager Man Singh asked that no one should move from their positions. As Srikkant recalled in his column, he was at that time standing outside the pavilion with a cup of coffee, and it was very cold. In one sweater, Srikkant remained rooted to his position for two hours, braving the chill, so that Kapil Dev could continue stroking the ball fluently and save India from disaster!

The impetus provided by that Herculean innings of Kapil Dev set the tempo for India's subsequent performance in that World Cup. India went on to win that match and create history by winning the World Cup 1983, too.

In the same World Cup, Mohinder Amarnath was man of the match in the semi-final against England and man of the match in the final against the West Indies, whom India defeated to become the World champions in 1983.

Recall that red handkerchief that used to peep out of his hip pocket. So did a red handkerchief peep out from the left pocket of the trousers of the tough Australian captain Steve Waugh. The red handkerchief was a gift to him from his grandfather.

Also, Waugh kept using the green baggy Aussie cap that was given to him on his debut. Though worn out after years of use, he used that cap in his last Test match too.

When the former Pakistan captain Imran Khan took the field in the final of the ICC World Cup 1992, against England,he wore the Tiger T-shirt. Imran took some bold decisions in batting and bowling and led Pakistan to the World Cup title.

Then we have the legendary Sunil Gavaskar, who used to

put on the left pad first while padding up for an innings. When he walked in to open the innings, he preferred that his opening partner was to his left.

Gavaskar was playing his last Test match in 1986-87 against Pakistan at Bangalore. His opening partner was Krish Srikkant, who preferred that his partner walked to his left. While going in to bat in the second innings, which was to be Gavaskar's last innings in a Test match, Gavaskar requested Srikkanth to allow him to walk to his right while openning the innings. Srikkant could not refuse that request and Gavaskar went on to play one of the greatest Test innings on a turning track. He missed his century by four runs, but even Imran Khan described that innings as one of the best.

Gavaskar had another ritual that he followed religiously while getting ready for innings. When putting on his pads, he liked to be left alone. He did not allow anyone to talk to him. He started concentrating from that moment itself.

Srikkant, besides preferring to walk to the right of his partner, looked upwards toward the sun, and always put on his left pad first. Sachin Tendulkar too prefers to put on the left pad first.

There is an interesting story related to Sachin Tendulkar and former India leg spinner Anil Kumble. When Kumble took all the ten wickets in an innings against Pakistan, there was an interesting superstitious ritual going on in that innings. Sachin Tendulkar would give Kumble's cap and sweater to the umpire, and Kumble would take another wicket.

Then there was former India captain and chief selector Dilip Vengsarkar, who did not shave on the day he was to bat.

Another former captain, whom Geoffery Boycott called the Prince of Calcutta, Sourav Ganguly, carried the photograph of his *Guru* and wore pendants round his neck. Before taking strike he would look inside the front of his shirt.

Dashing left handed batsman Yuvraj Singh, who hit Stuart Broad for six sixes off the six consecutive balls in an over in the T20 World Cup match against England, had a black thread round his wrist, reportedly on the advice of his mother as 'it would ward off evil eyes'. Young batting star Virat Kohli sports a black wristband.

Left arm fast bowler Zaheer Khan is known to carry a yellow handkerchief in crucial matches. Thus, we see that cricketers, from any country or continent, look for that something "extra" to sustain their self-belief. Such a superstitious streak touches Dhoni too. He said in an interview that he does not eat sweets on the match days. He does not want his parents come to the stadium to watch him play. Hence, despite their son being captain of Team India, Dhoni's parents have never been to a stadium to watch him play. His elder brother Narender refused to talk about the final or Dhoni before the match on the plea that if he did so it would bring bad luck.

One might add his visit to the Deori temple before every important tour or tournament for that something "extra" to sustain his self-belief. This superstitious streak touched his in-laws too, who preferred to watch their famous son-in-law lead India to World Cup victory on television at their home in Calcutta, instead of watching him live at Wankhede.

***

26 Dhoni-Annihilator or Finisher?

Should Dhoni go back to the role of an annihilator of the opposition bowling attack, and set the pace of the innings by playing aggressively from the word go as he did in his early days in Team India? Like he batted when he hit those 148 runs against Pakistan on 5 April 2005, at Vizag, his first international century in an ODI. Or that record breaking, match winning 183 against Sri Lanka at Jaipur, which made him surpass Adam Gilchrist's record of highest individual score by a wicketkeeper batsman. Incidentally, in both these innings he batted at number three.

In the same category would come his 148 runs against Pakistan at Faisalabad in 2006, which was his first Test century as well. Team India was in deep trouble having lost five wickets for 281 runs while chasing Pakistan's huge first innings score of 588 runs. Coming in at number seven, his lucky number, he was aggression personified. He bludgeoned the Pakistani attack, and doused the fire of their pace attack, when he hooked Shoaib Akhtar off his face for a six. It reminded many of us how Sachin Tendullar had blunted the Pakistani pace attack in the semi-final of the ICC Cricket World Cup, 2003, in South Africa by hitting Shoaib Akhtar for a six while collecting 18 runs from one over. That over set the tone of India's innings, though Sachin missed a century. In Faisalabad, however, Dhoni went on to score 148 runs from 153 balls, a hectic pace for a Test innings, hitting four sixes and 19 fours, that too when normal cricketing strategy demanded, that a batsman play cautiously and consume time so that precious time was lost and the opposition was denied time to force a win. Dhoni in that innings re-wrote the normal batting strategy.

Or, should he continue to play the role of a finisher, who nudges the ball for 1s and 2s and steadies the floundering batting line up, and then change gear in the death overs to take his team to victory, or at least to a position of strength.

One of the best and recent examples of his role as a finisher was the unbeaten 91 runs off 79 balls that he scored in the ICC Cricket World Cup final against Sri Lanka at Wankhede. He played the role of a finisher to perfection by starting quietly and accelerating later in the innings and finishing off the match with a huge six off the Lankan fast bowler Nuwan Kulasekara.

Or, recall that ODI against Sri Lanka in Australia in the CB triangular series in 2008. In a must win match, India were in trouble after losing four wickets for 99 runs while chasing Sri Lanka's 238 runs for five wickets. Dhoni played sedately and responsibly while scoring a fifty, which, did not contain any four or six!

Too much was at stake for him in that CB triangular series in Australia. Remember, he received quite a bit of criticism for having opted for "young legs" in the ODI team, which meant that the selectors dropped former captains Sourav Ganguly and Rahul Dravid from the ODI and these two stalwarts had to return home after the Test series. Test team's captain Anil Kumble had already quit the one-day cricket. Among seniors, Sachin Tendulkar only remained behind in Australia. Sachin did vindicate his stature as the leading batsman in international cricket by scoring 117 and 91 runs in the first two matches of the finals of the series to enable India to win the first two of the three-match final.

Dhoni's stand in favour of "young legs" was vindicated when India won the CB series finals 2-0, defeating Australia in its own den.

But some do appreciate his newly adopted role of a finisher. They would recall how he consumed 159 balls in scoring a match saving 76 runs against England at Lord's in 2007. That is, he scored one run off more than two balls. It cannot be described as one of his best innings, at least in terms of fluency, as he played and missed a number of times, but did not lose his confidence and kept going. In value, though, it will rate as one of those innings that saved India from a certain defeat.

It was an innings that made his fans wonder: Was it the same Dhoni who had hit 148 runs off 153 balls, his first century in Test cricket, that too at the rate of almost a run a ball?

But that innings stretched the Indian innings to that moment when it rained and saved the match. In that innings Dhoni played and missed a number of times. His critics pointed out deficiencies in his batting technique. But he had stayed at the wicket and steadied his team's innings after five wickets were lost in scoring 145 runs while chasing a target of 380 runs in the 4th innings of the match. Captain Rahul Dravid must be grateful to that patient knock by Dhoni, which was a display of grit and determination rather than a dazzling range of shots.

India went on to win the series, 1-0, courtesy a win in the second Test at Trent Bridge. It was the first series win after Kapil Dev had led India to a series win against England in England in 1986. It had taken twenty two years to win a series in England!

It was during this series that Rahul Dravid announced that he did not want to continue with captaincy and the BCCI selectors chose Dhoni to lead the Indian team in the inaugural edition of the T20 World Cup 2007, in South Africa.

Many cricket experts attribute his role of a finisher to his elevation as captain of Team India, which has made him responsible. But those who played with him in his early days say he had already that streak in him, through he revealed it very rarely. "During matches played at Sayal, some days we would watch him play more defensively than he normally did. He would play forward and backfoot defensive shots, pat the ball for a single or two, for a long while before shifting to the aggressive mode," recalls former Ranji batsman Adil Hussain.

But yes, cricket fans want Dhoni who played big and power packed shots. They want him to hit sixes aplenty, like those ten sixes that he hit in his knock of 183 against Sri Lanka at Jaipur. Even in early days he was noticed for his big hitting. Organizers of tournaments like Sheesh Mahal in Dehradun, would notice him and make enquiries about him for his aggressive batting, his power-packed shots and the sixes.

His aggressive stroke play fired up the imagination of millions of fans, whose blood warmed up on seeing raw power behind those shots. His sixes, were hit flat and so hard that the ball swerved in the air on its way over the sight screen, and bowlers ducked for safety to avoid a bullet like straight drive. The fielders in the cover were left stranded, as the ball scorched the grass on its way to the boundry.

His aggression was different from that of Virendra Sehwag. With his long mane and aggressive batting he became a youth icon soon after cementing his place in the Indian ODI team. No surprises that he was adjudged the Youth Icon by MTV viewers in 2006. Across the cricket crazy country, his fan following swelled. So did the number of endorsements.

But the demands of Team India in the international arena have made him more sedate, and now he looks to consolidate the middle order, and guide his team to a safe score, or usher it to a win. In this role at times his batting gives the impression that he has forgotten those lofty sixes.

Back to the question, Dhoni an annihilator or a finisher? Sure enough, given his commitment to his team, as its leader he would choose the role of a finisher because he always plays to win. The mind of committed fans of Indian cricket would accept his choice. But our hearts would always long to see Dhoni annihilate the best bowlers in the world, use his trademark "helicopter shot" more often to dispatch the ball way beyond the boundary line, and preferably out of the stadium.

***